The gourmet's guide to
JEWISH COOKING

The gourmet's guide to
JEWISH COOKING

Bessie Carr & Phyllis Oberman

TREASURE PRESS

First published in Great Britain by Octopus Books Ltd

This edition published in 1983 by Treasure Press
59 Grosvenor Street
London W1

© 1973 Octopus Books Ltd

ISBN 0 907812 24 4

Printed in Singapore

pp. 2–3 Cholent, the Sabbath midday meal

Contents

Traditions of Jewish cooking

Jewish cooking traditions, stretching back nearly two thousand years, are based on a set of dietary laws established in Biblical times.

These laws are the foundation on which all Jewish cooking is built, irrespective of the country in which the cook is living.

Jewish cooking is, therefore, not like any single national cooking style.

The fascination of Jewish cookery is the way in which an enormous cookery repertoire has been created, with contributions from hosts of countries, while still retaining allegiance to the Jewish Dietary Laws.

The great variety in Jewish cooking stems in part from the travels of Jewish communities from country to country in the Middle East, Asia Minor and Europe.

Local ingredients were made use of and variations on familiar themes became distinctive dishes in their own right. The names of dishes varied according to the country of origin, i.e. Russian, Polish, Spanish, or Middle Eastern.

In a way, the Jewish dietary laws limit the types of foods which may be eaten and the ways in which they can be used. For example, shellfish, game birds and all pig products are forbidden, and milk and meat may not be cooked or eaten together. However, these restrictions (fully described in the summary of Jewish dietary laws which follows),

allied as they are to a rich Jewish culture and life style, have had the reverse of a restrictive effect on this cooking tradition.

In fact, they have acted as a challenge to the ingenuity of hospitable Jewish housewives throughout the ages.

As well as adapting traditional Jewish dishes to the available raw materials, such as vegetables, fruits, fish, in whichever country they were domiciled, the Jewish cooks took local indigenous dishes and made them distinctly 'Jewish' in character. For example, the Viennese 'Apple Strudel' is seen by many today to be a Jewish dish, and 'Borsht', the Jewish beetroot soup, is now made without the meat stock of its Russian ancestor.

Jewish cooking is intimately tied to the Jewish religion. Because of the home-based nature of the Jewish religion, there is a universal interest in food and cookery, in home-produced (as opposed to shop-bought) food and a love for entertaining—for a 'celebration'—of which there are literally hundreds of traditional occasions.

At certain periods in Jewish history, particularly at the times of the ghettos in Europe from the Middle Ages onwards, the majority of Jews lived as underprivileged poor. Poverty fostered ingenuity— the talent of making a little food go a long way. That is why there is such a wide range of delicious

stuffed dishes in the Jewish cooking tradition—
from Holishkes (cabbage leaves stuffed with
minced meat) to Gefillte Fish (stuffed carp). These
dishes stretched expensive foods with cheap fillers,
while retaining the flavour of the costly food.
Now, in the twentieth century, these cleverly
devised dishes are the delicacies served on special
occasions for festivals and celebrations.
When these 'poor' dishes were originated the
Jewish housewife was rich in one commodity and
that was time, so many of these dishes were
laborious and time-consuming.
Now, the canning and freezing industries make
them optionally available to the modern housewife
via the Kosher counter in her supermarket or
freezer shop.

Shavuoth (Cheesecake)

Cholent

On the Jewish Sabbath (Saturday) no cooking or
other work is done by observant Jews, this day
being a true day of rest. From this came one of
the most famous Jewish dishes—Cholent.
This complete meal-in-a-pot is a long-cooking
casserole which commences cooking in a slow oven
before the eve of Sabbath (dusk on Friday night)
and which is just ready for lunch on Saturday.
Particularly in the colder countries of Eastern
Europe, a hot lunch was essential. The main
ingredients of Cholent are butter beans, potatoes,
onions, seasoning, a little expensive meat, and
sometimes a large dumpling cooked with it.
This dish, high in overall energy value, is another
example of a little meat being made to go a long
way. Modern nutritionists expound the value of a
small amount of meat protein with the additional
protein from cheap beans, an advantage hit upon
through necessity by generations of Jewish cooks.
Chicken is high in popularity in the Jewish
cuisine. One of the reasons for this goes back again

to the time when many Jewish communities were
confined to ghetto areas in European towns.
To raise beef or lamb requires green fields and
farms. All that is needed to raise chickens is a
small back yard, and so chickens, easily reared and
easily slaughtered, provided a convenient and
regular source of protein for the diet.
Many favourite Jewish dishes are associated with
religious festivals with which the year is studded,
and have seasonal or symbolic connotations. They
are so numerous because Judaism is a complete
way of life and takes place largely at home.
For example, we have Honey Cake at Rosh
Hashanah (New Year), Cheese Cake at Shavuoth
(Festival of Weeks) and Hamantaschen at Purim
(Feast of Esther), and a multitude of dishes at
Pesach (Passover) that contain no leaven.

*Pesach/Passover biscuits (around
edge of dish: Macaroons; centre
left: Cinnamon balls; centre right:
Coconut biscuits)*

In this book we give the authoritative information
required to prepare the recipes according to Jewish
custom in the accepted Kosher fashion.
We also hope that the contents will be of equal
interest to the non-Jewish cook who, perhaps, has
had a taste of this fascinating cooking tradition
and would like to explore it further.

Dietary laws

The Jewish Dietary Laws (Kashrut) are based on various edicts in the Torah (the first five books of the Old Testament) and consist of certain verses from Exodus, Deuteronomy and Leviticus.

Fish
only certain fish, those that have both fins and scales, may be eaten.

Birds
domestic poultry, i.e. chicken, duck, goose, turkey, and their eggs may be eaten.

Animals
certain animals, only those that chew the cud and have cloven hooves, may be eaten. The animals and poultry must be slaughtered in a special manner (Shechita), purged of certain veins and fat, and sold under recognized Rabbinical supervision.

To ensure that the meat and poultry have been prepared correctly, always buy at a shop displaying the sign which is the registered trade mark of the National Council of Shechita Boards in Britain, or another recognized Rabbinate abroad. All meat, poultry and liver must be koshered as below before placing in any utensil or into the freezer—even though it will have been bought from a kosher butcher.

To kosher meat
This should be done as soon as possible after it is brought home. Immerse the meat or bones in cold water for 30 minutes in a bucket or deep bowl, e.g. enamel or plastic which is kept for this purpose only.

Remove the meat, etc. and place it on a wooden, plastic, or wire grid which allows free drainage and is kept for this purpose only. Leave it to drain for a few minutes and then sprinkle it with coarse salt on all sides. Leave for 1 hour. Make sure that drips from the meat never splash on any utensils and that the meat never falls back into the soaking water, as this would make the meat trefa, i.e. not permitted. After 1 hour, wash it thoroughly in cold water three times.

To kosher poultry
Remove the liver and kosher separately as given below.
The poultry should be drawn and the lungs removed before koshering as for meat.
Place the pieces of poultry hollow side down.
If the bird is to be cooked whole, salt inside very carefully as well as outside.
Eggs found in the poultry, even with shells, should be koshered with the poultry and used only in meat dishes.

To kosher liver
Cut open the liver with a knife kept specially for this purpose. If the liver is in thin slices make slits across the surface.
Rinse it well with cold water and sprinkle with salt on all sides.
Place the liver in a wire basket or on the grid of a grill pan, kept for this purpose only, so that blood can run away freely. Grill it until cooked on all sides. Wash it thoroughly. Liver should be grilled immediately after washing and sprinkling with salt.
Always wash and then wipe the koshering equipment with kitchen paper and store in a separate place in the kitchen.

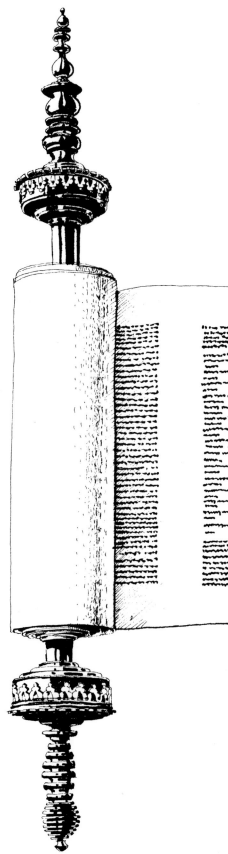

The scroll of the

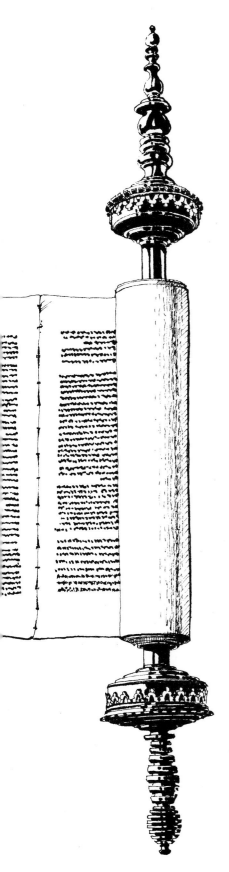

(Sefer Torah)

All recipes in the book using meat, bones, liver and poultry assume that they have been 'koshered' before use and, for the increasing numbers of freezer owners, they would be koshered before freezing, according to the directions given in this summary.

Eggs
should be broken separately into a glass and examined before using. If a blood spot is found, the egg should be discarded.

Vegetables and cereals
are permitted, but must be examined and cleaned to make sure that they are free from insects.

Milk and meat
may not be cooked or eaten together. Milk and meat dishes may not be placed in the oven at the same time. Quite separate and easily distinguishable sets of cooking utensils, china, cutlery, table linen, washing up bowls and working surfaces are required for meat and milk.

If at any time a mistake has been made by mixing meat and milk dishes or if there is any doubt about the foodstuffs, then a Rabbi should be consulted.

After eating meat foods, at least three hours should elapse before milk foods and milk beverages are taken.

Manufactured products
e.g. bread, biscuits, margarine, jellies, ice-cream and confectionery must be known to be free from non-kosher ingredients.

This can be assured by buying products manufactured under the supervision of the London Beth Din or another recognized Rabbinate. This applies also to washing-up materials. Information as to permitted washing-up liquids, scouring pads, etc. and information on foods in general can be obtained from the London Beth Din or its counterparts in other countries.

Special care must be taken to ensure that essences, colouring and cake decorations are made from vegetable or chemical ingredients only, ingredients to which there can be no objection in Jewish Law. When using chocolate for meat meals, make sure by asking your Rabbi or the Beth Din that the chocolate is free from milk products. So-called plain chocolate sometimes contains butter.

Kosher cheese
only should be used.

Kosher wines
only should be used.

Passover
as no 'leaven' may be eaten, only those foods (other than fresh fish, meat, poultry, eggs and most vegetables) should be bought that have been manufactured under the supervision of a recognized Rabbinate. Completely separate sets of milk and meat cooking utensils, crockery, cutlery etc., and koshering equipment are required and these should be stored away for the rest of the year.

Forspeisen

Forspeisen or starters—often savoury, salty or spicy—
are so popular in Jewish catering that several can be
combined to make a complete meal like supper.
In recent years, with the increased exports of fruits, such
as avocado pears from Israel, many variations have been
added to the more traditional dishes like chopped
herring.

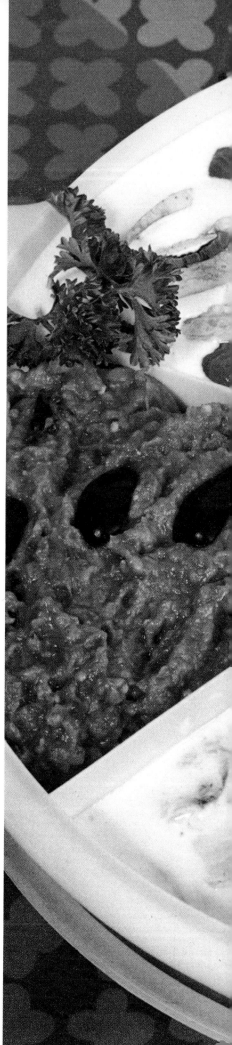

*bottom, anti-clockwise: Aubergine
[eggplant], eggs and onions;
Eggs and onions; Chopped
herring; Mushrooms in smetana;
Aubergine pâté; Herring salad*

10

Avocados

1 avocado pear (squeeze top to
see if it 'gives' and is ripe)
4 teaspoons lemon juice
½ teaspoon salt
¼ teaspoon pepper
parsley for garnish
serves 2

Cut the avocado pear in half, and remove the stone (pit). Mix all the other ingredients together, and pour over the two halves. Serve garnished with sprigs of parsley.

Avocado pear with celery, onion or leek

1 ripe avocado pear
1 small stick of celery, finely
chopped, or 1 teaspoon finely
chopped onion, or white part
of a leek
1 tablespoon (1¼T) olive oil
2 teaspoons lemon, or
orange juice
½ teaspoon sugar
½ teaspoon salt
¼ teaspoon pepper
parsley and olives for garnish
serves 2

Cut the avocado pear in half and remove the stone (pit). Place all the other ingredients in a small screw-topped jar, and shake well. Pour the mixture over two halves. Garnish with sprigs of parsley and olives.

Avocado pears with grapefruit and orange

4 avocado pears
½ teaspoon salt
4 teaspoons lemon juice
1 orange
1 grapefruit
8 black grapes
mint leaves for garnish

serves 8

Cut the avocado pears in half and remove the stones (pits). Mix the salt and lemon juice together and pour over the avocado pears. Peel the orange and grapefruit and divide into segments, removing all the pith.
Remove the pips from the grapes.
Arrange alternative segments of orange and grapefruit on the avocado pears. Garnish with the grapes and mint leaves. Pour any grapefruit and orange juice over the filled avocado pears.

Avocado surprise with tuna fish and cream cheese

1 avocado pear
2 tablespoons (2½T) tuna fish,
drained of oil
2 tablespoons (2½T)
cream cheese
1 tablespoon (1¼T) lemon juice
shake of pepper
parsley and black olives
for garnish
serves 2

Cut the avocado pear in half and remove the stone (pit). With a teaspoon, scoop out some of the flesh and place in a small bowl. Add the other ingredients and beat well. Pile the mixture into the avocado pear skins. Garnish with parsley and black olives.

Aubergine (egg plant) pâté

1 aubergine (egg plant)
½ teaspoon salt
⅛ teaspoon pepper
1 tablespoon (1¼T) mayonnaise
1 teaspoon lemon juice
1 teaspoon tomato purée
½ teaspoon finely chopped onion, or leek
lettuce, black olives, and parsley for garnish
serves 2–3

Wash the aubergine (egg plant). Wipe dry, pierce several times with a fork and grill gently on both sides, until soft. Or bake in the oven until soft, 400°F, Mark 6 for 20 minutes, depending on the size. Peel and place the flesh in a bowl, mix with the rest of the ingredients and beat well, or liquidize. Serve piled on the lettuce leaves, garnished with black olives and parsley.

note: this can be used as a dip.

Aubergine (egg plant), eggs and onions (Israeli 'chopped liver')

1 oz. (2T) margarine
1 onion
1 aubergine (egg plant)
½ teaspoon salt
⅛ teaspoon pepper
2 hard boiled eggs
lettuce and parsley for garnish

serves 4

Peel and slice the onion. Melt the margarine in a pan and fry the onions until soft. Wash, dry and grill the aubergine (egg plant) on all sides until soft, or bake in the oven, 400°F, Mark 6, for 20 minutes, according to size.
Mince (grind) the unpeeled aubergine (egg plant) and onions with 1 whole egg and 1 egg white. Add the seasoning and mix well. Arrange on lettuce leaves; sieve egg yolk over the aubergine (egg plant) mixture to decorate, and garnish with parsley.

Grapefruit and sour cream

1 grapefruit
2 tablespoons (2½T) sour cream
1 teaspoon sugar
2 glacé (candied) cherries, and mint leaves for garnish
serves 2

Cut the grapefruit in half and remove the flesh and place in a bowl. (Remove all pith.) Cut up the flesh of the grapefruit and mix with the sour cream and sugar.
Pile the mixture into the grapefruit cases (skins), decorate with the glacé (candied) cherries and mint leaves.

Felafel

8 oz. (1 good cup) chick peas
3 oz. (¾ cup) Matzo meal
2 eggs
1 teaspoon salt
2 teaspoons cumin
¼ teaspoon coriander
¼ teaspoon garlic salt
oil for frying
makes 3 dozen small balls

Soak the chick peas overnight. Mince (grind) the chick peas finely and add the other ingredients.
Shape into small balls and fry in deep oil until brown.
Serve hot with Techina sauce.

Techina sauce

2½ oz. (½ cup) ground sesame seeds
⅛ pint (¼ cup+1T) water
¼ teaspoon garlic salt
pinch cayenne pepper
pinch black pepper
¼ teaspoon salt
1 tablespoon (1¼T) lemon juice

Place all the ingredients in a liquidizer (blender) for a few minutes. Adjust the seasoning.

Avocado surprise with tuna fish
and cream cheese (opposite)

left: Soup Garnishes: Kneidlach (left);
Kasha (top); Mandlen
(bottom)

Avocado soup (below)

Eggs and onions

1 large onion
2 tablespoons (2½T) chicken fat,
or 1 oz. (2T) margarine
4 hard boiled eggs
salt and pepper to taste
lettuce, parsley, and tomato
serves 4

Peel and slice onion and fry gently in the fat until soft but not brown. Mince (grind) the fried onion and eggs together. Season with salt and pepper and mix well.
Serve on lettuce leaves, garnished with parsley and tomato slices.

note: if a very mild Spanish onion is used, it can be minced (ground) raw with the eggs and then mixed with the fat.

Chopped herring

2 salt herrings (for pickling) or
3 pickling herrings from a jar
1 Schmaltz herring
1 small Spanish onion
1 large cooking apple
2 hard boiled eggs
1 slice of bread
1–2 tablespoons (1¼–2½T)
vinegar or to taste
1–2 tablespoons (1¼–2½T) sugar
or to taste
serves 6–8

Skin and bone the herrings; or soak the pickling herrings overnight; rinse well.
Peel the onion and apple. Put the herrings, onion, apple, 2 whites of egg, 1 yolk of egg, and bread through the mincer (grinder). Add 1 tablespoon (1¼T) vinegar and sugar, and mix well. Add more sugar and vinegar if necessary to taste.
Serve sprinkled with sieved egg yolk.

Herring salad

2 pickled herrings
1 eating apple
¼ pint (⅔ cup) sour cream
lettuce leaves, paprika and
chopped parsley
serves 4

Remove the skin and bones from the herrings, and cut into small pieces. Peel and chop the apple (skin may be left on if liked). Mix the herring and apple with the sour cream. Serve on lettuce leaves, garnish with paprika and chopped parsley.

Mushrooms in smetana

4 oz. green grapes
4 oz. (1 cup) button mushrooms
½ pint (1¼ cups)
creamed smetana
2 teaspoons lemon juice
pinch salt and pepper
a few shredded lettuce leaves
chopped parsley and paprika
serves 2

Remove the skin from the grapes by pouring boiling water over them, then dipping them into cold water. Cut in half and remove the pips (seeds). The skin can be left on if desired. Wash and slice the mushrooms very finely.
Mix the grapes and mushrooms into the smetana. Add the lemon juice, salt and pepper.
Divide the shredded lettuce into 4 glasses. Place a portion of the mixture in each glass, and sprinkle with chopped parsley and paprika. Or serve in an hors d'oeuvre dish.

Tuna fish cocktail

1 × 7 oz. can tuna fish
1 teaspoon finely chopped onion
1 teaspoon lemon juice
3 tablespoons (3¾T) mayonnaise
1 teaspoon tomato purée
shake of pepper
6 stoned black olives
4–6 lettuce leaves
parsley, paprika and 4
lemon slices
serves 4

Drain the tuna fish and discard the oil. Mix the onion, lemon juice, mayonnaise and tomato purée together. Add the pepper and 4 chopped olives. Add the tuna fish in pieces and mix gently.
Shred the lettuce, and place in 4 glass goblets. Add the tuna fish mixture, garnish each with a black olive, parsley, and shake of paprika.
Place a lemon slice on the rim of each goblet.

Tuna fish cocktail

Petcha (calf's foot jelly) (right)
Schwartz retaych (black radish)
(far right)

Petcha or footsnoga Calf's foot jelly

1 calf's foot or ½ ox foot
1 onion
2 cloves garlic
1 bayleaf, optional
½ teaspoon peppercorns, optional
salt and pepper to taste
2 tablespoons (2½T) lemon juice
2 hard boiled eggs
lemon and parsley to garnish

Have the calf's foot chopped into several pieces and clean it well. Peel and slice the onion. Chop the garlic. Put the foot, onion, garlic, bayleaf and peppercorns, if used, and seasonings into a pan. Cover with cold water. Simmer for about 3 hours, until the meat drops from the bones. (In a pressure cooker this will take about 1 hour.)
Remove the meat and cut into small pieces. Strain the liquid. Add the lemon juice and adjust the seasoning as required, and mix with the meat.
Pour into a shallow dish, add slices of egg and when cool, place in the refrigerator.
When serving, garnish with lemon slices and parsley.

Gehackte leber Chopped liver

1 large onion
2 tablespoons (2½T) chicken fat
or margarine
4 oz. chicken livers or tender
ox liver
2 hard boiled eggs
salt and pepper
lettuce, tomato and parsley
for garnish
serves 3—4

Peel and slice the onion, fry in the fat until soft and pale brown; add the liver and fry for a further 1 or 2 minutes. Mince (grind) the onion, liver, 1 whole egg and the white of the second egg. Add salt and pepper and mix well.
Arrange on lettuce leaves; garnish with sieved egg yolk and with tomato and parsley.

note: the crisp pieces of skin left over when the chicken fat is rendered can be minced (ground) with the liver, or served as a garnish with the chopped liver.

Schwartz retaych   Black radish

8 oz. black radish—3 small ones **1 small mild onion, optional** **salt and pepper to taste** **1 tablespoon (1¼T) chicken fat** **lettuce** serves 3–4	Peel and grate the black radish. Grate the onion finely. Mix the onion, radish and seasoning with a sufficient amount of chicken fat to bind. Serve on lettuce leaves.

Sweet and sour giblets

1 tablespoon (1¼T) chicken fat
or margarine
2 sets of giblets
1 onion
1 carrot
1 stick of celery
2 teaspoons brown sugar
juice of lemon and ¼ teaspoon
finely grated rind of lemon
¼ pint (½ cup+2T) stock or
¼ pint (½ cup+2T) water and
1 kosher chicken stock cube
1 teaspoon tomato purée
1 teaspoon cornflour (corn
starch) mixed with 2 tablespoons
(2½T) cold water
parsley for garnish
serves 4

Melt the fat in a pan and fry the chopped giblets until brown. Remove. Peel and chop the onion, carrot and celery and fry together until the onion is soft. Add the sugar and cook for 1 minute to darken. Add the lemon juice and rind, stock and purée. Replace the giblets and cook until tender, for about 1 hour.
Add the blended cornflour (corn starch); bring to boil, stirring all the time. Adjust the seasoning. Serve sprinkled with chopped parsley. Plain boiled rice can be served with this dish.

Buckling Lightly smoked herring

1 buckling
juice of ½ lemon
½ Spanish onion
lettuce leaves
serves 1

Skin and bone the buckling. Sprinkle with lemon juice. Cut the onion into very thin rings.
Serve the buckling on lettuce leaves and garnish with the onion rings.

Soups

Despite slimming regimes soups, in most Jewish households, still maintain their popularity. Soup has no status symbol and is served regularly with everyday meals in Jewish homes. Two of the most famous Jewish soups are Goldene Yoich (Chicken Soup)—few Friday Night (eve of Sabbath) meals exclude it—and Borsht (Beetroot Soup).

Avocado soup

1 heaped teaspoon cornflour
(cornstarch)
1 pint (2½ cups) chicken stock
(or 1 pint (2½ cups) water and
2 stock cubes)
1 avocado pear (about ½ lb.)
1 teaspoon lemon juice to taste
salt and pepper to taste
serves 2–3

Blend the cornflour with 2 tablespoons (2½T) stock. Place the rest of the stock in a pan and bring to the boil, pour over the blended cornflour (corn starch), return to the pan and cook thoroughly. Place the stock in a liquidizer (blender) with the peeled and stoned (pitted) avocado pear; add the lemon juice and seasoning. Liquidize until smooth. Adjust the seasoning. Reheat if necessary, but do not boil. If you do not have a liquidizer, sieve the avocado pear into the stock.

Borsht

1 lb. beetroots
1 large onion
1 cooking apple
1 lemon
2 pints (5 cups) water
1 teaspoon salt
1 teaspoon sugar
¼ lb. new potatoes, optional
1 egg yolk mixed with 2
tablespoons (2½T) cold water
serves 4

Peel the beetroot, onion and apple and cut up very small. Add the grated rind of half a lemon and juice of half a lemon. Cover with the water. Add 1 teaspoonful of salt and sugar.
Cook until almost tender, about 1 hour. Add the scraped potatoes and cook until all are tender. Strain, keeping potatoes if used.
Season with more lemon juice, sugar and salt if necessary. Place the egg in a large basin, and gradually beat in the borsht. Add the potatoes and serve warm or quite cold.
If reboiled, borsht will curdle.
Can be served with a swirl of sour cream.

Barley and bean soup

1 onion
1 carrot
1 stick celery
1 oz. (2T) chicken fat
or margarine
2 oz. (¼ cup) barley
2 oz. (¼ cup) butter or haricot
beans, soaked overnight
2 pints (5 cups) stock, or water
and meat bones
salt and pepper
parsley for garnish
serves 4

Peel and grate the onion, slice the carrot and celery. Melt fat in a pan and sauté the vegetables. Add the washed barley, beans, stock, or water and bones, and seasoning.
Cook gently for 2 hours or until the beans are tender. Adjust the seasoning, remove the bones and serve the soup with chopped parsley.
A pressure cooker can be used.

Hubagrits soup
Oats and vegetables

1 oz. (2T) chicken fat
or margarine
1 large onion
1 large carrot
1 stick celery
1 small turnip
1 teaspoon salt
⅛ teaspoon pepper
2 pints (5 cups) stock, or water
and meat bones
2 oz. (¼ cup) hubagrits (oats)
parsley for garnish
serves 4

Prepare vegetables, grate the onion and chop the carrot, celery and turnip. Melt the fat in a saucepan. Add the vegetables and fry until soft. Add the seasoning, stock, or water and bones, and well rinsed hubagrits. Bring to the boil and cook gently until the soup is thick, about 2½ hours. (Remove bones, if used.) Serve garnished with chopped parsley.

note: a pressure cooker can be used.
Graplech (cracked wheat) can be used instead of hubagrits.

Lentil soup

1 oz. (2T) margarine
1 carrot
1 piece turnip
1 onion
1 stick celery
2 pints (5 cups) stock or water
seasoning
pinch dried herbs or bouquet garni
4 oz. (½ cup) lentils
1 heaped teaspoon cornflour
(cornstarch) blended with 2
teaspoons cold water
parsley or fried cubes of bread

serves 4

Prepare the vegetables and slice. Melt the fat in a pan. Add the vegetables and fry until soft. Add the stock, or water and bones, seasoning, herbs and lentils.
When the vegetables are tender (about 1 hour) sieve the soup, or liquidize. Add the blended cornflour (cornstarch), boil thoroughly. Adjust the seasoning.
Serve with chopped parsley or fried cubes of bread.
Cornflour (cornstarch) may not be needed if soup is liquidized.
A pressure cooker can be used.

Sweet and sour cabbage borsht with raisins

1 lb. (3½ cups) grated Dutch or red cabbage
1 grated (1½ cups) raw beetroot
2 pints (5 cups) water
2 teaspoons salt to taste
1 tablespoon (1¼T) sugar to taste
2 teaspoons acetic acid
4 oz. (1 cup) raisins
1½ oz. (3T) margarine
1½ oz. (⅜ cup) flour

serves 6

Place the cabbage, beetroot, water, salt, sugar and acetic acid in a saucepan. Bring to the boil. Add the raisins. Cook for 1 hour or until vegetables are soft.
Melt the margarine in a separate pan, add the flour and cook until brown. Remove from the heat. Pour a little of the soup on to the flour and margarine, stirring all the time. Add up to ½ pint (1¼ cups) of the soup and bring to the boil. Add the sauce mixture to the cabbage soup at end of the cooking time. Adjust the seasoning by adding more salt, sugar or acetic acid as required.

variations:

1. Use lemon juice instead of acetic acid.
2. Use stock instead of water (or add 2 stock cubes).
3. Use 1 pint (2½ cups) tomato juice instead of 1 pint (2½ cups) water.

Sweet and sour cabbage borsht with raisins

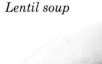

Lentil soup

Split pea and worsht

1 onion
1 carrot
1 piece of turnip
1 stick of celery
1 tablespoon chicken fat
4 oz. (½ cup) split peas,
soaked overnight
1 teaspoon salt
¼ teaspoon pepper
2 pints (5 cups) stock
4 oz. worsht
1 heaped teaspoon cornflour
(corn starch) blended with 2
tablespoons (2½T) water
extra worsht and lochshen
for garnish
serves 4

Prepare and chop the vegetables. Melt fat in a pan and fry vegetables until brown. Add the soaked peas, seasoning and stock. Bring to the boil, add the worsht cut into pieces. Cook for 2 hours or until soft. Sieve or liquidize. Thicken, if necessary, by adding the blended cornflour (corn starch). Bring to the boil and cook thoroughly. Garnish with extra worsht or chopped lochshen.
A pressure cooker may be used.

Asparagus soup

½ oz. (1T) butter
½ small onion
1 medium tin (about
8 oz.) asparagus
milk to add to liquid in tin, to
make 1 pint (2½ cups)
½ teaspoon salt ⎫
pinch of pepper ⎬ to taste
1 level tablespoon cornflour
(corn starch) blended with
2 tablespoons (2½T) cold water
¼ teaspoon Marmite, or other
vegetable extract
2 tablespoons (2½T) water
1 yolk of egg mixed with 2
teaspoons cold water
2 tablespoons (2½T)
cream, optional
parsley for garnish
serves 2–3

Peel and chop the onion. Melt the butter in a saucepan and cook the onion slowly. Add most of the asparagus, leaving the remainder for the garnish. Add the liquid, bring to the boil and cook for 10 minutes. Add the blended cornflour and cook for 1 minute, stirring all the time. Add the Marmite.
Liquidize, or pass through a sieve. Pour over the beaten egg yolk, stirring slowly all the time. Reheat but do not boil, adjust the seasoning. Serve garnished with asparagus tips and chopped parsley.

Split pea and worsht soup

Asparagus soup

24

Smetana soup

½ pint (1¼ cups) smetana
1 tablespoon (1¼T) chopped radishes
1 tablespoon (1¼T) chopped spring onions (scallions) or chives
1 tablespoon (1¼T) chopped cucumber
squeeze of lemon
pinch of salt
2–3 tablespoons (2½–3¾T) top-of-the-milk (light cream)
paprika
parsley for garnish
serves 2–3

Mix together the smetana, radishes, onions, cucumber, lemon juice and salt. Add the top-of-the-milk (light cream) to thin down, if necessary. Serve in individual dishes. Sprinkle with paprika. Garnish with chopped parsley.

Smetana soup

Tschav, green borsht, or sorrel soup

1 lb. sorrel leaves
2 pints (5 cups) water
1 onion
1 teaspoon salt
½ teaspoon lemon rind
juice of 1–2 lemons, to taste
1–2 oz. (⅛–¼ cup) sugar, to taste
1 egg yolk mixed with 2 tablespoons (2½T) cold water
serves 4

Wash the sorrel leaves and remove any thick stalks. Prepare and finely chop the onion. Place the sorrel leaves, water, onion, salt, rind and juice of 1 lemon and 1 tablespoon (⅛ cup) of sugar in a saucepan. Cook until tender, about 20 minutes. Cool a little and then very slowly pour on to the beaten egg yolk. Adjust the seasoning. Serve chilled.
Boiled new potatoes can be served with the borsht. They can be cooked in it.
Sour cream can be added as a garnish.

Fruit soup

1 lb. black cherries or plums
juice of lemon and rind of ¼ lemon
2 oz. (¼ cup) sugar
2 pints (5 cups) water
¼ teaspoon salt
2 level tablespoons (2½T) cornflour (cornstarch)

Place the washed cherries or plums in a saucepan with the lemon juice and rind, sugar, water and salt. Bring to the boil and simmer until tender. Press through a sieve to remove the stones.
Blend the cornflour (cornstarch) with 4 tablespoons (5T) of cold water. Pour into the soup, and cook until boiling, stirring all the time. Adjust the seasoning. Chill and serve with sour cream, if liked.

note: canned fruit can be used, in which case omit sugar during cooking.

variations:
1. Mixture of apples and blackberries.
2. Rhubarb, using orange juice and rind instead of the lemon.
3. Apricots.
4. Add 2–3 (2½–3¾T) tablespoons red wine.

serves 4

Quick tomato soup with rice

2 pints (5 cups) chicken stock,
or 2 pints (5 cups) water and
2 chicken stock cubes
¼ pint (½ cup+2T) tomato purée
1 teaspoon sugar
½ teaspoon lemon juice
pinch of sweet basil
pinch of mace
1 bay leaf
2 oz. (good ¼ cup) long
grained rice
serves 4

Place all the ingredients in a saucepan. Bring to the boil and cook for 15 minutes, or until the rice is soft. Remove the bay leaf and adjust the seasoning. Serve with extra rice if liked.

Schwemelach (dried mushroom) and barley soup

½ oz. (1T) margarine or
chicken fat
1 onion
1 carrot
1 stick celery
1 small piece turnip
2 pints (5 cups) stock
1 teaspoon salt
⅛ teaspoon pepper
¼ oz. (1T) dried mushrooms
(well rinsed)
2 oz. (¼ cup) barley (well rinsed)
serves 4

Prepare the vegetables, grate the onion and chop carrot, celery and turnip. Melt the fat in a pan, add onion, carrot, celery and turnip. Fry gently until all the fat has been absorbed. Add the stock, seasoning, mushrooms, and barley, bring to the boil. Reduce the heat and simmer for about 2 hours until the soup is thickened by the barley.
A pressure cooker can be used.

*Schwemelach (dried mushroom)
and barley soup*

Goldene Yoich

1 boiling fowl; 1 or 2 sets of giblets can be used instead
1 large onion
2 carrots sliced lengthwise
piece of parsley root
1 stick of celery
1 teaspoon salt
¼ teaspoon pepper
water to cover
parsley for garnish

Remove all the fat from the scalded fowl. Prepare and slice the vegetables. Put the fowl in a large saucepan, and add the vegetables and seasoning. Cover with water. Bring to the boil. Remove the scum. Simmer for about 3 hours or until tender (or pressure cook according to manufacturer's instructions).

Remove the fowl and serve it separately. Skim the soup to remove the fat. Adjust the seasoning, and sprinkle with chopped parsley. Serve with lochshen or other soup accompaniments.

Noodle squares

1 egg
¼ teaspoon salt
pinch of pepper
3 oz. (¾ cup) plain (all purpose) flour
serves 3–4

Beat together the egg, salt and pepper. Gradually mix in sufficient flour to form a fairly stiff dough. Roll out the dough, cut into ½ in. squares and leave to dry.

Cook in boiling, salted water. Cook for 5 minutes, strain and serve in soup.

Kasha

1 egg
½ teaspoon salt
pinch of pepper
6 oz. (1 cup) buckwheat groats (kasha)
1¼ pints (3 cups) boiling water or stock

Beat the egg with the salt and pepper and stir into the kasha. Place in a thick based saucepan and stir over gentle heat to set the egg. Add the boiling water, and cook until all the water has been absorbed and grains are tender. A little more water may be required to prevent sticking.

variations: kasha can be served as a soup accompaniment or to make savoury dishes as follows:
1. Serve with a rich gravy as an accompaniment to a pot roast.
2. Mix with fried onions and mushrooms and serve as an accompaniment to chicken or meat.
3. Kasha with varishkes—Mix with 1 large onion, fried in 4 tablespoons (8T) chicken fat, and cooked noodle squares. Minced (ground) grieven (crisp pieces of skin when rendering chicken fat) can also be added.

serves 6–8

Meat balls

8 oz. minced (ground) meat
1 egg
pinch of pepper
1 teaspoon very finely grated onion
pinch of garlic salt
makes about 16

Mix all the ingredients together. Form into very small balls. Drop into the boiling soup. Reduce the heat, and cook for 15 minutes. Drain and serve in soup.

Particularly good in a tomato soup, or with chicken soup and lochshen.

note: meat balls can be fried and served at buffets on cocktail sticks.

Einlauf

1 egg
4 tablespoons (5T) water
pinch of pepper
¼ teaspoon salt
3 oz. (¾ cup) plain (all purpose) flour
serves 3–4

Mix together the egg, water, salt and pepper. Add this mixture to the flour. Beat well.

Drop a thin stream of the mixture into boiling soup. Reduce the heat and cook for 2–3 minutes. Drain and serve in the soup.

Lochshen

1 egg
¼ teaspoon salt
pinch of pepper
3 oz. (¾ cup) plain (all purpose) flour, approximately
serves 3–4

Beat together the egg, salt and pepper. Gradually mix in sufficient flour to form a fairly stiff dough. Roll out very thinly and leave to dry. Roll up tightly, and then cut into thin strips.
Cook in boiling, salted water, separating the strips as they are put into the water. Cook for 5 minutes, strain and serve in soup.

Bread kneidlach

1 tablespoon (1¼T) chicken fat
1 onion
2 oz. (1 cup) white breadcrumbs
1 egg
½ teaspoon salt
pinch of pepper
makes about 16 balls

Peel and grate the onion. Melt the fat in a saucepan and fry onion until brown. Mix together the fat, onion, breadcrumbs, eggs, salt and pepper. Beat well with a fork. Form into small balls. Drop into boiling soup and cook for 5 minutes.

Kneidlach

1 small onion
2 tablespoons (2½T) melted chicken fat
4 oz. (1 cup) medium matzo meal
salt and pepper
¼ pint (½ cup+2T) boiling water
1 egg
makes about 24

Peel and grate the onion. Melt fat in a saucepan and fry the onion. Add to the matzo meal with the salt and pepper. Add the boiling water, and allow to cool, then add the beaten egg. Stir well. Leave in the refrigerator to chill thoroughly.
Dip your hands into cold water and then roll the mixture into tiny balls. Drop the balls into the boiling soup or boiling, salted water and simmer gently for 15 minutes.
Serve in soup.

Mandlen

1 egg
1 tablespoon (1¼T) oil
½ teaspoon salt
3 oz. (¾ cup) plain (all purpose) flour

Mix together the egg, oil and salt. Add the sifted flour to make into a dough.
Form into pencil thin ropes on a floured board, with floured hands. Cut into ¼ in. pieces.
Bake in the oven on a greased tin at 375°F, Mark 5, for 15–20 minutes until brown, shaking gently after 10 minutes.

note: thinner mandlen can be obtained by rolling the ropes of dough thinly, cutting into tiny squares; leaving to dry for 30 minutes and then frying.

variations: deep fry in oil, remove with a slotted spoon and drain on
serves 4 absorbent kitchen paper.

Farfal

1 egg
pinch of pepper
½ teaspoon salt
4 oz. (1 cup) plain (all purpose) flour
serves 3–4

Mix the egg and seasoning together. Add enough flour to make a very stiff dough. Set aside for about 1 hour to get hard, and then grate coarsely. Spread out the farfal thinly to dry (these can be put in a very cool oven to hasten the process).
To use, sprinkle into boiling, salted water or soup.
Cook for 5 minutes and then drain.

Bread kneidlach

Fish

Jewish housewives are discriminating fish buyers. In a Jewish home no-one eats simply 'fish', but haddock, herring, plaice, sole, hake, halibut, salmon, carp and many others.

According to Jewish Dietary Laws all fish which have scales and fins may be eaten, giving the cook a very wide variety from which to choose. Fish may be eaten at the same meal with meat but never on the same plate or cooked in the same dish.

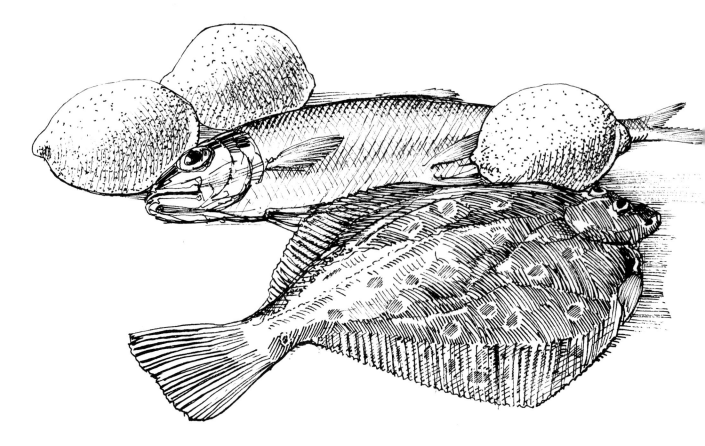

Spiced fish

2 lb. haddock, cod, or hake;
fish can be left whole, or if
preferred, filleted, skinned, and
cut into serving pieces
½ teaspoon salt
1 onion
1 clove garlic, or ¼ teaspoon
garlic salt
1 green pepper
2 bay leaves
¼ pint (½ cup+2T) tomato purée
⅛ pint (¼ cup) oil
2 tablespoons (2½T) lemon juice
parsley for garnish

serves 4

Sprinkle the fish with salt. Place the fish in a greased baking dish.
Peel and finely chop the onion and garlic. Remove the seeds from
green pepper and slice finely. Place the onion, garlic, green pepper,
pepper, and 2 bay leaves on top of the fish. Blend together the purée,
oil and lemon juice and pour over fish.
Cover the dish with foil. Bake in the oven at 350°F, Mark 4, for 45
minutes. Remove the bay leaves. Serve garnished with chopped
parsley.

Halibut with egg and lemon sauce

1 slice halibut, about 1 lb.
1 onion
1 carrot
¼ pint (½ cup+2T) water
salt and pepper
juice and rind of ¼ lemon
parsley and lemon slices
for garnish

sauce:
2 level teaspoons cornflour
(cornstarch)
1 lemon

serves 2

Wash the fish. Prepare the onion and carrot, slice and place in a
shallow saucepan or frying pan. Place the washed fish on top of the
vegetables, add water, seasoning and lemon rind.
Cover with a lid or large plate. Bring to the boil and cook very gently
for about 15 minutes. When fish is opaque it is cooked. Very carefully
lift out the fish and place on a dish. Strain the liquid left in the
saucepan.

sauce: blend the cornflour (cornstarch) with strained lemon juice.
Bring the fish stock to the boil and pour over the blended cornflour
(cornstarch), return to the pan and cook for 1 minute. Allow the
mixture to cool a little and then pour it over the beaten egg. Pour
the sauce over the fish and decorate with sprigs of parsley and lemon
slices.

note: sugar to taste may be added to sauce if liked.

Gefillte fish

2 lb. fish—a mixture is best:
white fish, such as carp,
haddock, cod, and whiting; rich
fish, such as herring, mackerel,
bream (only use about ½ lb. of
rich fish)
1 carrot
3 medium sized onions
2 teaspoons salt
pepper
3 tablespoons (3¾T) matzo
meal, or white breadcrumbs
1 teaspoon sugar
2 eggs

serves 4

Ask the fishmonger to fillet and skin the fish, but take bones, head
and skin; wash fish, bones and skin for making the stock.
Prepare and slice carrot and onion. Put the fish bones, head, skin,
carrot, 1 onion, 1 teaspoon of the salt and a shake of pepper into a
pan and cover with water. Cook for about 20 minutes.
Mince (grind) the fish with the other two onions, and the bread, if
used. Mix together with the salt, pepper, sugar, and beaten eggs and
matzo meal, if used.
With wetted hands, make the mixture into 14–16 balls and place them
in the fish stock. Simmer gently for 1 hour or longer. Remove the fish
balls from the stock, place on a plate and decorate with slices of the
cooked carrot. Strain the stock, chill and serve separately.

note: these fish balls may be fried instead of boiled.
Gefillte fish is really stuffed fish (usually carp) and to do this the fish
has to be cut down the back to remove the flesh and leave the
underpart whole. Cut into slices and place fish balls in each slice.
Cook as above.

Baked stuffed fish

4 cod, hake or haddock steaks
1 oz. (2T) melted margarine
2 teaspoons grated onion and
chopped parsley
beaten egg or milk to bind
4 tablespoons (5T) breadcrumbs
or matzo meal
salt and pepper
pinch of mixed herbs, optional
squeeze of lemon
serves 4

Remove the bone from the fish. Mix together all the ingredients for the stuffing. Fill the hollow in the fish. Place stuffed fish in a greased dish and cover with buttered paper. Bake in the oven at 400°F, Mark 6, until tender, about ½ hour.
Remove the fish and place on a hot dish. (Save liquor (liquid) for sauce.) Pour round tomato and black olive sauce.

Tomato and black olive sauce

½ oz. (1T) margarine
1 grated onion
½ tablespoon (¾T) flour
1 small tin of tomatoes
4 tablespoons (5T) white wine
or 1 teaspoon lemon juice and
liquor (liquid) from the fish
pinch of sugar
2 oz. (⅓ cup) black olives
seasoning

Melt the margarine in a pan, add the onion and cook until brown. Add the flour and cook for 1 minute. Add the chopped tomatoes, wine and liquor from the fish. Add the sugar, bring to the boil and simmer for a few minutes. Add the chopped stoned (pitted) olives. Adjust the seasoning.

Fried fish

suitable fish—haddock, cod,
hake, plaice, sole or herring
salt
beaten egg
fine matzo meal
oil for frying
parsley or lemon slices

According to size, the fish may be filleted or cut into slices. Wash and drain the fish, and season with salt to taste.
Dip the fish into the beaten egg and then into the fine matzo meal. Press the matzo meal firmly on to the fish and shake off any surplus. Heat the oil (360°F). Place the fish carefully in the oil and fry until golden brown. Turn it over and cook the other side. Drain on crumpled absorbent paper. Decorate with lemon slices or sprigs of parsley. The fish may be served hot with chips (French fries), or cold with salad.

Scharfe fish

2 lb. haddock, hake or cod, cut
into 4 serving slices
1 teaspoon salt
1 teaspoon peppercorns
2 tablespoons (2½T) lemon juice
1 sliced carrot
1 sliced stick of celery
1 chopped onion
⅜ pint (1 cup) water
1 oz. (2T) margarine or butter
1 oz. (2T) flour
1 egg yolk mixed with 2
teaspoons cold water
serves 4

Sprinkle the fish with salt. Place the peppercorns, lemon juice, carrot, celery, and onions in a saucepan with the water and bring to the boil. Add the fish, bring to boil again, then reduce the heat and simmer for about 10–15 minutes until fish is opaque and tender. Remove the fish on to a heated serving dish and keep hot.
Melt the margarine in a small saucepan, add the flour and cook for half a minute. Remove from the heat and gradually stir in strained fish liquor. Bring to the boil, stirring all the time. Pour the sauce over the egg yolk. Adjust seasoning. Pour the sauce over the fish.

Sweet and sour mackerel

1 lb. mackerel
1 carrot
1 onion
½ teaspoon salt
2 teaspoons sugar
1 tablespoon (1¼T) lemon juice
2 level teaspoons cornflour
(cornstarch)
yolk of egg mixed with 2
teaspoons cold water

serves 2

Wash and clean the fish, cut off head and cut into pieces (2 or 3 according to size of fish). Prepare and slice carrot and onion. Place in a saucepan with the onion, carrot, sugar, salt, and just cover with water. Bring to the boil and then cook gently for about 15 minutes until fish is tender and opaque. Remove the fish from saucepan and place on dish. Strain the fish liquor.
Blend together the lemon juice and cornflour (cornstarch). Pour the hot liquor over the blended cornflour (cornstarch). Return to the pan, bring to boil and cook for 1–2 minutes. Adjust seasoning. (It is important to taste the sauce and add more lemon juice, sugar or salt to get the correct flavour.) Pour the sauce slowly over the beaten yolk, beat well. Pour over the fish.

Sweet and sour mackerel

Halibut with egg and lemon sauce

Gefillte fish (right)
Spiced fish (below)

Bream in cream sauce

2 lb. bream, filleted and skinned
2 tablespoons (2½T) flour
shake of pepper
¼ teaspoon salt
1 oz. (2T) margarine and 1
tablespoon (1¼T) oil
¼ lb. (1 cup) mushrooms
4 tomatoes
1 teaspoon lemon juice
¼ pint (1 cup) single
(light) cream

Wash and dry the fish. Mix the flour with the seasoning. Cut the fish into serving pieces and toss in the seasoned flour. Heat the margarine and oil in a frying pan and cook the fish gently on both sides until opaque, about 10 minutes. Remove to a serving dish and keep hot. Wash and dry the mushrooms, slice and place with the halved tomatoes in the frying pan. Cover and cook gently for 10 minutes. Arrange the mushrooms and tomatoes around the fish. Pour the lemon juice into the frying pan, add the cream, and heat until nearly boiling, stirring all the time, and add the seasoning. Pour over fish, and serve at once.

Salmon patties

1 medium tin salmon (7½ oz.)—
pink will do
1 egg
1 small onion, grated
2 tablespoons (2½T) matzo meal
⅛ teaspoon pepper
oil for frying
makes about 5 patties

Mix all the ingredients together, beat well. Shape into flat cakes. Fry on both sides in hot oil. Drain and serve.

Salmon patties (right)

Soused herring (far right)

Salmon mayonnaise

2 lb. salmon
½ teaspoon salt
pinch of pepper
1 teaspoon lemon juice
1 slice of onion
lettuce, slices of lemon,
cucumber, tomatoes and hard
boiled eggs for garnish

serves 4

Place the salmon on an oiled sheet of foil. Sprinkle on both sides with salt, pepper, and lemon juice. Add the onion. Close the foil. Place in a saucepan with sufficient cold water to cover the parcel of fish. Bring to the boil and reduce the heat until the water is barely simmering and cook for 10 minutes. Leave to cool in liquor. Remove from the saucepan, and skin the fish. Serve on a plate garnished with lettuce, lemon, cucumber, tomatoes and hard boiled eggs. Serve the mayonnaise separately.
The salmon may also be served hot with new potatoes and peas.

Mayonnaise

1 egg yolk
pinch of pepper, mustard and
salt
1 dessertspoon (1T) lemon juice,
or vinegar
¼ pint (½ cup+2T) olive,
groundnut or corn oil
2 teaspoons boiling water

Place the egg yolk in a basin with the seasonings. Beat very well, and add ¼ teaspoon vinegar or lemon juice. Gradually beat in the oil, a drop at a time, to prevent curdling. When thick add the rest of the lemon juice or vinegar. To give a lighter texture add 2 teaspoons of boiling water at end.

Soused herring (or mackerel)

1 onion
2 herrings or mackerel
½ teaspoon sugar
½ teaspoon salt
shake of pepper
1 teaspoon pickling spices
1 bay leaf
vinegar and equal amount of
water to cover fish
lettuce

serves 2

Peel and slice the onion. Wash, trim and bone the fish. Place an onion slice on each fish and roll up from the head to the tail. Secure with a cocktail stick (toothpick) and place in a pie dish. Add the rest of the onion, seasoning, pickling spices, and bay leaf. Pour over sufficient vinegar and water mixture to cover the fish. Cover pie dish with foil.
Bake for ¾ hour in the oven at 400°F, Mark 6. Allow to cook in liquor. Remove the fish and pat dry on kitchen paper. Serve on lettuce leaves.

Meat and poultry

In most countries only the forequarters meat of beef, lamb or veal is available from kosher butchers. This means that the most tender cuts of meat are not offered for sale and those cuts which can be grilled or fried amount to only a very small part of the forequarters. So traditionally, most meat dishes are designed for long, slow cooking.

Veal casserole with dumplings

Gedempte fleisch

2 tablespoons (2½T) chicken fat
or margarine
2 lb. flap, chuck steak, brisket,
flank, or top rib
¼ teaspoon garlic salt
2 onions
2 carrots
1 stick celery
½ tablespoon (¾T) tomato purée
¼ teaspoon sugar
½ teaspoon salt
¼ teaspoon pepper
¼ pint (½ cup+2T) stock

thickening einbren
1 tablespoon (1¼T) chicken fat
or margarine
1 tablespoon (1¼T) flour
serves 4–5

Melt the fat in a heavy pan. Add the meat and crushed garlic, or garlic salt, and brown meat on all sides. Remove to a plate. Prepare and chop the vegetables. Add to the pan and fry gently, until brown. Replace the meat. Mix together the tomato purée, sugar, salt, pepper and stock, and pour over the meat. Cover the pan tightly. Bring to the boil, and then simmer for 2½ hours or until tender. Place the meat on a serving dish, and keep warm.

Melt the chicken fat in a small saucepan, add the flour and cook until pale brown. Remove the pan from the heat and add the skimmed, sieved liquor (liquid) from the meat, a little at a time, stirring well. Bring to the boil and pour some over the meat; serve the rest separately.

Mustard casserole

2 lb. beef—chuck steak, flap,
or flank
1 tablespoon (1¼T) flour
½ teaspoon mustard
shake of pepper
clove of garlic, or ¼ teaspoon
garlic salt
1 oz. (2T) margarine or
chicken fat
1 onion
1 carrot
1 stick celery
small piece of turnip or swede
a few mushrooms, if liked
¼ pint (½ cup+2T) stock
1 lb. potatoes, or a few slices
of challah spread with chicken
fat, or margarine, and mustard
serves 4–5

Cut the meat into cubes and remove the fat. Dip the meat in flour mixed with mustard and pepper. Melt fat in a pan and fry meat and crushed garlic until brown. Remove the meat. Prepare and chop the vegetables. Fry in the pan until onion is soft. Place the meat and vegetables in a casserole. Pour off any excess fat from pan, add liquid and bring to the boil, add to the casserole.

Peel, slice and sprinkle the potatoes with salt. Cover contents of casserole with sliced, salted potatoes, or bread spread with mustard. Cover tightly and cook for at least 2 hours in the oven at 350°F, Mark 4. Half an hour before serving, remove the lid to brown the potatoes or bread.

Mustard casserole (right)
Gedempte fleisch (opposite above)
Braised bola (opposite below)

Braised bola

1 oz. (2T) margarine or
chicken fat
2 lb. round bola
½ teaspoon garlic salt
2 onions
2 carrots
1 stick celery
pinch of pepper
¼ pint (½ cup + 2T) stock
1 teaspoon cornflour (corn
starch) blended with 2
tablespoons (2½ T) cold water

serves 4–5

Melt the margarine in a frying pan. Add the meat and brown on all sides. Remove the meat and put on one side. Prepare and chop vegetables into large pieces. Add the vegetables and crushed garlic, or garlic salt, to the pan and fry slowly. Place the vegetables in a casserole and add the meat. Add the pepper and stock to the pan. Bring to boil and pour over the meat. Cover the casserole tightly and cook in the oven at 325°F, Mark 3, for 2½–3 hours.

Slice meat and place on a hot dish with the vegetables. Skim the fat from the liquor left in the casserole, and pass liquor through a sieve or liquidizer. Mix with blended cornflour (cornstarch), bring to the boil and cook thoroughly; serve separately.

Goulash

2 lb. chuck steak
1 oz. (2T) margarine, chicken fat, or oil
2 onions
2 level teaspoons paprika
pinch of caraway seeds
½ pint (1¼ cups) tomato juice and a stock cube, or 3 tablespoons (3¾T) tomato purée, or ½ lb. skinned tomatoes and just under ½ pint (1¼ cups) of stock
¼ teaspoon sugar
1 lb. potatoes, optional
serves 4–5

Cut the meat into cubes. Peel and slice onions. Melt fat in a pan and fry meat until brown, then add the onions. Cook for a few minutes, then add all the other ingredients except the potatoes. Cover and simmer until tender, about 2 hours. (Tomatoes vary in flavour so add additional purée if necessary.) Adjust seasoning.

Prepare and slice potatoes. Half an hour before the meat is cooked, slice the potatoes, sprinkle them with salt and add to the meat.

Rossel fleisch

2 lb. chuck steak
2 tablespoons (2½T) chicken fat
1 clove garlic, or ¼ teaspoon garlic salt
2 onions
2 carrots
¼ pint (½ cup+2T) water
1 bone
¼ teaspoon pepper
serves 4–5

Cut the meat into 4 servings. Melt the fat in a saucepan, and fry the meat until brown on both sides, set aside. Add the crushed garlic or garlic salt.
Prepare and chop the vegetables. Fry the vegetables in the pan until the onion is soft. Add the water, bone, pepper and meat, and cover closely. Bring to the boil, and then reduce the heat and simmer for 2 hours until the meat is tender. Remove the bone and adjust the seasoning.
Serve with potato latkes.

Goulash (above left) *Rossel fleisch and potato latkes (above right)*

Rouladen

1½ lb. prime bola cut in 2 long slices
1 tablespoon (1¼T) chicken fat
2 cloves garlic, crushed, or ½ teaspoon garlic salt
1 onion, chopped
1 carrot, chopped
1 stick celery, chopped
½ pint (1¼ cups) stock
pinch of pepper
1 rounded teaspoon cornflour (cornstarch) blended with
2 tablespoons (2½T) water

stuffing
1 tablespoon (1¼T) chicken fat
1 oz. (¼ cup) matzo meal
1 teaspoon grated onion
shake of pepper
1 large pickled cucumber, grated
1 egg

serves 4

Cover the meat with a sheet of plastic and then beat out meat until very thin with a rolling pin. Cut each piece into 2. Make the stuffing by mixing all the stuffing ingredients together. Place a portion on each piece of meat, roll up and secure with cocktail sticks. Melt fat in flameproof casserole and fry the rouladen until brown all over. Set aside.

Fry the garlic and vegetables in the same fat until pale brown. Add the stock and pepper to the casserole, bring to the boil, and replace the rouladen. Cover casserole tightly and cook for 1½ hours in the oven at 350°F, Mark 4.

Remove the rouladen to a hot serving dish. Liquidize or sieve the vegetables and gravy. If liked, the gravy can be thickened by adding the blended cornflour (cornstarch) to the liquidized gravy and reboiling. Adjust the seasoning.

Serve rouladen coated with some gravy. Serve the rest of the gravy separately.

Serve with mashed potatoes.

Sauerbraten

2 lb. top rib, or flap, or brisket
$\frac{1}{8}$ pint ($\frac{1}{4}$ cup) vinegar
$\frac{1}{2}$ teaspoon garlic salt
1 tablespoon (1$\frac{1}{4}$T) finely
chopped onion
1 tablespoon (1$\frac{1}{4}$T) brown sugar
1 bay leaf
1 teaspoon mixed
pickling spices
1 tablespoon (1$\frac{1}{4}$T) chicken fat
$\frac{1}{8}$ pint ($\frac{1}{4}$ cup) stock
serves 4–5

Place the meat in a glass dish. Mix together the vinegar, garlic salt, onion, sugar, bay leaf and pickling spices. Pour over the meat, cover and leave in a refrigerator overnight or even for 1 day. Drain the meat and wipe dry.

Heat the chicken fat in a flameproof casserole, and brown the meat all over. Add the strained marinade and stock, cover the casserole closely and cook in the oven at 325°F, Mark 3, for 2$\frac{1}{2}$–3 hours.

Essigfleisch

2 lb. brisket, flap, top rib
2 tablespoons (2$\frac{1}{2}$T) chicken fat
2 onions
2 carrots
2 tablespoons (2$\frac{1}{2}$T) brown sugar
grated rind of $\frac{1}{2}$ lemon
juice of 1 lemon
$\frac{1}{2}$ pint (1$\frac{1}{4}$ cups) stock
extra sugar and lemon juice
serves 4–5

Cut the meat into serving pieces. Melt the fat in a pan and brown the meat and remove to plate. Prepare and chop the onions and carrots, add to pan and fry until brown. Add the sugar and cook until it darkens a little. Add the lemon rind and juice and stock, and replace the meat.

Bring to the boil. Cover the pan tightly and simmer for 2 hours until tender. Adjust the seasoning. Serve with fresh bread.

Meat blintzes

4 oz. (1 cup) flour
pinch of salt and pepper
2 eggs
$\frac{1}{2}$ pint less 2 tablespoons (1$\frac{1}{4}$
cups less 2$\frac{1}{2}$T) water
oil for frying

filling
Any of the meat fillings used for
kreplach or pirogen
serves 3–4

Mix together the flour and seasoning. Add the eggs and water and beat until smooth with a rotary whisk.

Heat a few drops of oil in a pan. Pour in a little batter, tilting the pan so that a film of batter covers the pan. Fry until set.

Turn the pancake on to a plate, panside up, and place a tablespoon (1$\frac{1}{4}$T) of the filling in the centre. Roll up the pancake and tuck in the ends.

Place in a greased baking dish and brush with oil. Repeat until the batter is finished. Bake in the oven at 400°F, Mark 6, for 30 minutes. These pancakes can be fried gently on both sides in a little oil.

Lamb and babilach casserole

2 lb. neck of lamb or breast
of lamb
1 oz. (2T) margarine or
chicken fat
1 onion
1 carrot
piece of turnip
4 oz. ($\frac{1}{2}$ cup) haricot beans
(pea beans), soaked overnight
$\frac{1}{2}$ teaspoon salt
shake of pepper
pinch of dried
rosemary, optional
2 tablespoons (2$\frac{1}{2}$T)
tomato purée
$\frac{1}{2}$ pint (1$\frac{1}{4}$ cups) stock
serves 5–6

Cut the meat into pieces and remove excess fat. Prepare and slice the vegetables. Melt the fat in a pan and fry the meat and the vegetables until brown; pour off excess fat. Add the beans, stock, seasoning and purée. Bring to the boil and simmer for 2 hours; or place in casserole and cook in the oven at 375°F, Mark 5, for 2 hours.

Sliced potatoes can be placed on top if desired.

Moussaka

3 aubergines (egg plants)
2 teaspoons salt
5 tablespoons (6¼T) oil
1 onion, chopped
1 lb. (2 cups) minced (ground) lamb
2 tablespoons (2½T) tomato purée
¼ teaspoon garlic salt
¼ teaspoon pepper
¼ teaspoon mixed herbs
4 level tablespoons (5T) cornflour (cornstarch)
1 pint (2½ cups) stock
2 eggs mixed with 1 tablespoon (1¼T) cold water

serves 6

Peel the aubergines (egg plants) and cut into thin slices, and sprinkle both sides with salt. Place on a large plate, cover with another plate, and place a weight on top. Leave for 30 minutes. Heat 1 tablespoon (1¼T) of oil and fry onion until soft. Add the meat and fry for a few minutes, then add the tomato, garlic salt, pepper and herbs. Continue to cook gently, with lid off so that all liquid evaporates.

Rinse the aubergines (egg plants), pat dry on absorbent paper and fry gently in the pan until brown in the rest of oil, using more oil if necessary. In well-greased oven dish, place a layer of aubergines (egg plants), then a layer of meat. Repeat, ending with a layer of aubergines (egg plants).

Blend the cornflour (cornstarch) with 8 tablespoons (1½ cups) of stock. Bring the rest of the stock to the boil, pour over blended cornflour (cornstarch), return to pan and cook thoroughly. Allow the mixture to cool slightly and pour over the well beaten egg. Adjust the seasoning and pour over the mixture in the oven dish. Bake in the oven at 325°F, Mark 3 for 1 hour.

To give a crisp topping, breadcrumbs can be sprinkled on top and dotted with margarine.

Baked worsht potatoes (left)
Braised liver with mushroom and rice (above)
Roast duck (below)
Moussaka (opposite)

Veal casserole with dumplings

2 lb. neck or breast of veal
½ oz. (1T) margarine, chicken fat or oil
1 onion, chopped
½ oz. (1T) flour
½ pint (1¼ cups) stock, or water and a stock cube, or half stock and half red wine
4 oz. (1 cup) mushrooms
pinch of dried herbs
pinch of cloves
¼ teaspoon pepper
¼ teaspoon salt

Cut the meat in pieces. Melt the fat in a pan and brown the meat with the onions. Remove the meat from the pan and place in a casserole. Add the flour, stirring well. Add the stock and wine, and bring to the boil. Add the mushrooms, herbs and seasoning, and pour over the meat.
Cover the casserole and cook in the oven at 325°F, Mark 3, for 1½ hours. Add dumplings and cook covered for another ½ hour.

Dumplings

4 oz. (1 cup) self-raising flour
pinch of salt, pepper and mixed herbs
1 oz. (2T) margarine
cold stock or water

Mix together the flour and seasonings. Rub in the margarine. Mix to a fairly stiff dough with the stock or water. Form into balls and place on the meat in casserole; replace lid.

Klops Minced meat loaf

2 lb. minced (ground) meat
1 carrot, grated
1 onion, grated
¼ teaspoon garlic salt
⅛ teaspoon pepper
⅛ teaspoon celery salt
4 tablespoons (5T) water or stock
2 teaspoons tomato purée
2 eggs
2 tablespoons (2½T) white breadcrumbs or matzo meal
serves 5—6

Mix all the ingredients together very well. Place in a well greased loaf tin. Cover with foil.
Bake in the oven at 350°F, Mark 4, for 1½ hours. The foil can be removed during last half hour to brown the meat.
Serve hot with mushroom sauce, or cold with salad.

Mushroom sauce

4 oz. (1 cup) mushrooms
1 teaspoon grated onion
2 oz. (4T) margarine
1½ oz. (3T) flour
¾ pint (2 cups) stock
salt and pepper to taste

Wash and slice the mushrooms. Melt ½ oz. (1T) margarine in a saucepan and cook mushrooms and onion gently together. Remove on to a plate. Heat the rest of margarine in the saucepan. Add the flour and cook a few seconds. Remove from the heat, and add the stock, a little at a time. Bring to the boil, and cook thoroughly, stirring all the time. Add the mushrooms, and reheat. Adjust the seasoning.

Koklaten I

1 lb. (2 cups) minced (ground) meat
1 onion, grated
1 tablespoon (1¼T) matzo meal
1 tablespoon (1¼T) chopped parsley
pinch of salt, pepper and garlic salt
1 egg
seasoned flour
oil
serves 2—3

Add the grated onion to the meat, then mix in the matzo meal and seasoning. Beat in the egg and shape into flat cakes. Dredge with seasoned flour.
Place a little oil in a baking tin and put in the meat cakes. Bake in a moderate oven at 375°F, Mark 5, for about 1¼ hours.
If onions are not liked, these can be omitted or served fried on top of Koklaten.

Koklaten II

1 lb. (2 cups) minced
(ground) beef
1 tablespoon (1¼T) grated onion
pinch of pepper
pinch of paprika
pinch of garlic salt
1 tablespoon (1¼T) water
oil for brushing
serves 2–3

Mix all the ingredients together. Form into flat cakes. Brush with the oil, then place under hot grill for 5 minutes, turn over and brush the other side with oil and grill for another 5 minutes. Serve with grilled tomatoes and mushrooms if liked.

These can be fried in hot oil or baked, see Koklaten I, page 48.

Pepper holishkes

4 large peppers
1 lb. (2 cups) minced
(ground) beef
4 oz. rice (½ cup)—long grained
rice is best
2 onions, minced
salt and pepper

sauce
⅛ pint (¼ cup+1T) tomato purée
1 onion, finely grated
1 teaspoon lemon juice
1 teaspoon brown sugar
salt
½ pint (1¼ cups) stock or water
serves 4

Cut the stems from the peppers and remove the seeds. Wash well. Wash rice. Mix the meat with the rice, onions and seasonings. Stuff the peppers with the mixture and put in a casserole.

Combine all the sauce ingredients and simmer gently for a few minutes. Adjust the seasoning, then pour over peppers. Cover and cook in the oven at 425°F, Mark 7, for 1 hour.

Pepper holishkes

Braised liver with mushroom and rice

1 oz. (2T) chicken fat
or margarine
1 tablespoon (1¼T) onion, grated
1 tablespoon (1¼T) flour
¼ teaspoon salt
pinch of pepper
½ lb. liver
½ lb. (2 cups) mushrooms
¼ pint (½ cup+2T) stock
6 oz. (1 cup) raw rice
parsley and paprika for garnish
serves 3

Melt the fat in a saucepan and cook the onion gently until soft. Mix together the flour, salt and pepper. Cut the liver into pieces, dip in the seasoned flour and fry gently with the onion. Wash and slice the mushrooms, add to the liver and cook for a few minutes. Add the stock, bring to the boil. Place in a casserole. Cover tightly and cook in the oven at 325°F, Mark 3, for ¾ hour.

Cook the rice in plenty of boiling, salted water until tender but not mushy. Strain and rinse in hot water. Press rice into a greased ring tin. Press down tightly, turn on to a dish and pour the liver and mushrooms into centre of the rice ring. Garnish with chopped parsley and paprika.

Stuffed breast of lamb

1–2 breasts of lamb, depending on size

stuffing
1 onion, grated
1 cooking apple, or ¼ lb. gooseberries, chopped
4 tablespoons (5T) matzo meal, or white breadcrumbs
a few mint leaves, chopped, or pinch of rosemary
1 egg
1 tablespoon (1¼T) melted chicken fat, or margarine
¼ teaspoon salt
shake of pepper
serves 2–3

Bone the meat and remove excess fat. Mix all the ingredients for stuffing together. Spread over the boned meat. Roll up and wrap in foil, and bake in the oven at 400°F, Mark 6, for 1½ hours. Open up the foil to brown meat for last ½ hour.
Serve hot with mint sauce.
If it is to be eaten cold, rewrap tightly in foil and cool. Refrigerate, then slice and arrange on platter garnished with lettuce, watercress, tomatoes and parsley.

Stuffed breast of lamb

To render chicken fat

½ lb. (1 cup) fat
⅛ pint (¼ cup+1T) water
1 onion, optional

Cut the fat into small pieces. Place in a pan with the water. Cover and place on a very low heat. When the fat is golden in colour and the water has evaporated, add the chopped onion. Fry until the onion is light brown. Pour off the fat and store in a jar.
Use the remaining crisp skin (grieven) as a side dish with chopped liver, or mince with liver.

Lung and liver pie

1½ lb. lung
1 onion
½ pint (1¼ cups) water
salt and pepper
1 onion, sliced
2 onions
2 oz. (4T) margarine or chicken fat
crushed clove of garlic or ¼ teaspoon garlic salt
½ lb. liver, minced (ground)
¼ pint (½ cup+2T) stock
1 level tablespoon (1¼T) flour
2 tablespoons (2½T) cold water

pastry
8 oz. (1 cup) margarine
12oz. (3 cups) plain (all purpose) flour
4 tablespoons (5T) water
serves 8

Rub the margarine into the flour. Make into a stiff dough with the water. Place the lung in a large saucepan with the sliced onion and ½ pint (1¼ cups) water, salt and pepper. Bring to the boil and simmer for about 1 hour, or pressure cook for 20 minutes. Allow to cool. Remove the skin and tubes and mince (grind).
Mince (grind) the 2 onions. Melt fat in a pan and fry onions until they are soft. Add the garlic, minced (ground) lung and liver and fry a few minutes. Add stock and more salt and pepper. Blend the flour with 2 tablespoons (2½T) of cold water, pour into mixture, simmer, stirring until the mixture thickens, allow to cool.
Cut the pastry into two pieces. Roll out one half thinly and line a baking dish with it. Dampen the edges. Spoon over cooled filling. Roll out the rest of the pastry and place over filling. Seal the edges. Brush with beaten egg, if liked. Bake in the oven at 425°F, Mark 7, for 20 minutes, turn oven down to 375°F, Mark 5, and cook for 20 minutes longer.
Usually lungs are sold as a 'set' of lungs and often weigh 2½–3 lb.

Calf's sweetbreads

2–3 calf's sweetbreads
salt and pepper
1 egg, beaten
matzo meal
oil for frying

Plunge the sweetbreads into boiling water for a few minutes, then into cold water. Remove the fat and the skin and press the sweetbreads between two plates with a weight on top until cold. Cut each sweetbread in half, season with salt and pepper. Dip into the beaten egg, then into the matzo meal. Heat oil in a frying pan (skillet) and fry sweetbreads until golden brown. Arrange on a hot dish.

Roast duck

duck (4–5 lb.)
salt and pepper
garlic (optional)
juice of 1 orange

stuffing
1 oz. (2T) chicken fat
1 small onion, chopped
2 oz. (½ cup) raisins, soaked in 2 tablespoons (2½T) hot stock
8 oz. (1⅓ cups) long grain rice (or 3 cups cooked rice)
1 apple, peeled and chopped
salt

Orange sauce
1 tablespoon (1¼T) flour
juice and rind of 1 orange
juice and rind of ½ lemon
¼ pint (½ cup+2T) stock
salt and pepper
serves 5–6

Melt the fat in a saucepan and fry the onions. Mix in the raisins, rice, apple and seasoning.
Season the duck with salt and pepper and rub the outside with the cut clove of garlic or sprinkle with garlic salt. Stuff the bird and place it on a rack in a baking tin. Pour the juice of the orange over and cover the breast with foil. Put in a hot oven at 425°F, Mark 6, for the first 15 minutes, then finish in a cooler oven at 375°F, Mark 4, removing the foil 30 minutes before it is ready (1½–2 hours, according to size).
Remove the duck and keep hot. Pour off the fat into a tin, except for 1 tablespoon (1¼T). Add 1 tablespoon (1¼T) flour and cook until brown. Add the juice and rind of 1 orange and ½ lemon and ¼ pint (½ cup + 2T) stock. Cook until thick, adjust seasoning. Strain into a gravy boat.
Stock can be made by boiling giblets, onion and seasoning.

Roast stuffed chicken

1 roasting chicken, weighing 4–5 lb.

stuffing
4 oz. (1 good cup) matzo meal or breadcrumbs
½ teaspoon salt
pinch of pepper
1 small onion, finely grated
crushed clove garlic, if liked, or shake of garlic salt
pinch of dried sage
2 tablespoons (2½T) melted chicken fat
1 egg
a little water
½ teaspoon garlic salt, or clove of garlic
salt and pepper
carrot, finely sliced
onion, finely sliced
serves 5–6

Mix together the meal or breadcrumbs, seasonings, onion, garlic and fat. Add the beaten egg and enough water to make a soft mixture. Use this to stuff the chicken, being careful to allow room for it to expand during cooking.

Stuff the chicken. Rub with a cut clove of garlic, or sprinkle with garlic salt, and sprinkle with seasoning.
Put the onion and carrot in the roasting tin. Place the chicken on top of them. Cover the chicken with foil. Cook for about 2–2½ hours in oven at 325°F, Mark 3, removing the foil for the last ½ hour, so that the chicken can brown.
Remove the bird to a hot dish and make the gravy.

gravy: remove the vegetables from the roasting tin. Pour off the fat, leaving 1 tablespoon (1¼T) in the roasting tin. Add a level tablespoon (1¼T) of flour and cook until brown. Add ½ pint (1¼ cups) of chicken stock, bring to the boil and cook well. Adjust the seasoning. Strain into a gravy boat.
The chicken can be basted with ¼ pint (½ cup + 2T) canned pineapple juice, and this can be used to make gravy instead of ¼ pint (½ cup + 2T) stock. Place rings of pineapple around the chicken to garnish.

Stuffed chicken neck (helzel)
(right)
Boiled ox tongue, or Salt beef
(opposite)

Stuffed chicken neck helzel

1 neck of chicken
3 tablespoons (3¾T) flour
salt and pepper
1 tablespoon (1¼T) raw chicken fat

Mix together the sifted flour and seasonings. Add the fat cut into small pieces. Mix well.
The quantities will need to be varied a little to suit the size of the neck.
Scald the neck, scrape and rinse it. Sew up one end with white thread. Stuff loosely and sew up the other. Cook in boiling soup, or boiling salted water, or cook with a casserole of chicken or cholent.

Baked worsht potatoes

1 large potato
4 slices frying worsht

serves 1

Scrub the potato and prick with a fork. Make 4 cuts in the potato but not right through. Insert the worsht in the cuts. Cover completely with aluminium foil. Bake in a hot oven at 425°F, Mark 6, for about 1 hour until potatoes are cooked.
Serve with mustard and whole tomatoes. If liked each piece of worsht can be spread with a little mustard before baking.

Spiced braised veal

2 lb. breast of veal, boned and rolled
2 tablespoons (2½T) chicken fat or margarine
1 carrot
1 stick of celery
1 onion
¼ pint (½ cup+2T) stock
½ teaspoon mixed pickling spices and 1 bay leaf tied in a muslin bag
grated rind of ½ lemon
¼ teaspoon pepper
crushed clove of garlic, or ¼ teaspoon garlic salt
1 teaspoon cornflour (cornstarch) blended with 2 tablespoons (2½T) cold water

serves 4–5

Melt the fat in a pan and fry the meat until brown; place in a casserole. Prepare and slice the vegetables, and fry in the pan until onions are soft. Place the vegetables in the casserole, pouring off any excess fat. Add the stock, seasonings and bag of spices to the pan and bring to the boil. Add to the casserole. Cook closely covered for 2 hours in the oven at 325°F, Mark 3.
Remove bag of spices. Remove the meat and keep hot. Press the vegetables and liquor in the casserole through a sieve or liquidize (blend). Add the blended cornflour (cornstarch) to liquidized vegetables, bring to the boil, adjust the seasoning. Serve as a sauce with the meat.

Boiled ox tongue (or salt beef)

1 salted ox tongue or salt beef
2 bay leaves
1 onion
1 carrot

Wash the meat. Let cold water run over it for a few minutes. Put the meat in a large saucepan with cold water to cover. Prepare and slice vegetables. Add vegetables and bay leaves to pan. Bring to the boil. Remove the scum as it arises. Simmer for about 2½–3 hours until tender. (Or pressure cook according to manufacturer's instructions.) When cooked, pour cold water over the tongue. Remove the skin and gristle, and any excess fat at the root end. Serve either hot or cold. To serve cold, place the meat on a sheet of foil, wrap very tightly and place a weight on top. When cool, store in the refrigerator. Serve thinly sliced, with salads.

To salt (pickled) beef and tongue

about 3 lb. brisket or tongue; flap or flank can also be pickled
4 pints (10 cups) water
½ lb. (1 cup) coarse salt
¼ oz. (2 teaspoons) saltpetre
1 oz. (2T) brown sugar
teaspoon of mixed pickling spice, optional

Heat the water, add all the ingredients, except the meat, stir to dissolve the salt and sugar and leave to cool. Place the meat in a deep dish, pour over the strained pickling solution. Put a heavy plate on top to keep meat under surface of the liquid. Cover dish with muslin. A tight lid should not be put over it.
Store in a cool place for about 7–10 days.

Wiener schnitzel

4 thin pieces of veal for schnitzel, weighing 1 lb.
1 egg
seasoned flour
fresh breadcrumbs
oil for frying

Flatten the veal with a rolling pin, until really thin, between 2 sheets of cellophane.
Dip in the seasoned flour, then in beaten egg, and finally in breadcrumbs, pat well. Fry in hot oil until golden brown each side, about 3–4 minutes.
Serve with wedges of lemon.
Veal cutlets can also be cooked in this way.

seasoned flour: 3 tablespoons (3¾T) of flour mixed with ⅛ teaspoon salt and ⅛ teaspoon pepper.

serves 4

53

Egg, cheese and dairy dishes

Cream cheese and sour cream were, until recent years, traditionally made in the home, and their ready availability explains the mass of dishes containing these items in Jewish cookery. Orthodox Jews only bought kosher hard cheese, which is slightly less popular in cooking.

A typical breakfast in modern-day Israel includes a jug of sour milk or 'leben' which is drunk by the glass and served with slices of cheese, slivers of fresh vegetables, such as cucumbers and green peppers, and bread.

Mammaliga

¾ pint (2 cups) water
½ teaspoon salt
1 oz. (2T) butter
5 oz. (1 scant cup) cornmeal
3 oz. (¾ cup) grated cheese
1 oz. (2T) butter for 'dotting'

serves 3–4

Bring the water, salt and butter to the boil. Sprinkle the cornmeal over the water, stirring all the time. Cook until thick, simmering gently.
Turn out onto a flat board, leave until cool. Cut into squares. Place in well greased baking dish, cover with the grated cheese, dot with the butter and bake for 30 minutes in the oven at 375°F, Mark 5, to brown.

Mushroom and cheese filling for blintzes

4 oz. (1 cup) mushrooms
1 oz. (2T) butter
1 teaspoon grated onion
4 oz. (1 cup) grated cheese
salt and pepper to taste

serves 4

Wash and slice the mushrooms. Melt the fat in a pan; add the onion and sliced mushrooms, and cook gently with lid on. Cook until soft for about 5 minutes. Add the grated cheese and seasoning.
To make blintzes, see page 78.

Lochshen kaese and puter

¼ lb. (1½ cups) thick lochshen (vermicelli)
1 teaspoon salt
about 2 pints (5 cups) water
½ lb. (1⅓ cups) curd (cottage) cheese
1 oz. (2T) butter
extra butter, sugar and cinnamon, if liked

serves 3–4

Cook the lochshen in boiling salted water. Drain. Mix with the butter and cheese, reheat. Serve immediately with extra butter, sugar and cinnamon, if liked.

top: *Lochshen kaese and puter;*
bottom: *Lochshen kaese kugel*

Lochshen kaese kugel

¼ lb. (1½ cups) broad lochshen
1 teaspoon salt
about 2 pints (5 cups) water
1 oz. (2T) butter
½ lb. (1⅓ cups) curd cheese
½ tablespoon sugar
½ tablespoon sultanas (white raisins), if liked
5 oz. (1 cup) sour cream or smetana

serves 4

Boil the lochshen in salted water until cooked but still firm. Rinse in cold water and drain well. Add the butter, cheese, sugar, and half the sour cream (or smetana). Place in a well greased oven dish, pour over rest of the sour cream, or smetana. Bake in the oven at 350°F, Mark 4, for 20 minutes.

Tuna and egg roll

filling
1½ oz. (3T) margarine
1½ oz. (3T) flour
½ pint (1¼ cups) milk
½ tablespoon (¾T) vinegar
1 tablespoon (1¼T) capers
1 tablespoon (1¼T)
gherkin, chopped
1 × 7 oz. can tuna fish
2 hard boiled eggs
½ teaspoon salt
¼ teaspoon pepper
1 teaspoon onion, finely chopped

pastry
6 oz. (1½ cups) plain (all
purpose) flour
4 oz. (8T) margarine
2 tablespoons (2½T) water
serves 6

Melt the margarine in a saucepan, add the flour and cook for 1 minute, but do not brown. Remove the pan from the heat. Slowly add the milk, stirring all the time. Return to the heat, bring to the boil and cook until thick. Add the vinegar, capers, gherkins, well drained and flaked tuna fish, chopped eggs, salt and pepper. Spread on a plate to cool.

Make the pastry by rubbing the margarine into flour until it resembles fine breadcrumbs and mix it to a dough with the water. Roll out the pastry into an oblong about 16 × 8 in. Place the filling in a strip along middle of the pastry and wet the edges of the pastry. Fold the pastry to meet in the middle, seal the edges. Place on a greased tin, brush with milk. Bake in the oven at 425°F, Mark 7, for 30 minutes.

Tuna and egg roll (right)
Stuffed aubergine (egg plant)
(opposite)

Cheese kreplach

1 egg
salt and pepper
about 3 oz. (¾ cup) plain (all
purpose) flour

filling
8 oz. (1⅓ cups) curd cheese
1 egg
2 tablespoons (2½T)
sugar, optional

Beat the egg with the seasonings. Gradually beat in enough plain (all purpose) flour to form a stiff dough. Roll the dough out very thinly and leave it to dry for about 1 hour. Cut into 3 in. squares. Make the filling. Mix all the ingredients together. Beat well. Place teaspoonsful of the mixture on each square; wet the edges and fold them over to form a triangle. Seal the edges and then press the two longer points together. Leave to dry for 30 minutes. Drop into gently boiling water and simmer for about 15 minutes. Drain and serve with melted butter.

Stuffed aubergine (egg plant)

1 aubergine (egg plant)
½ level teaspoon salt
2 tablespoons (2½T) oil
1 onion, chopped
2 oz. (⅔ cup) breadcrumbs
a little grated lemon rind
salt and pepper
2 oz. (½ cup) grated cheese
1 egg

serves 2

Cut the aubergine (egg plant) in half, lengthways. Run a knife just inside the skin and score the flesh with a knife. Sprinkle with salt and leave for 30 minutes. Drain off any liquid and pat with absorbent paper.

Heat the oil in a pan and cook the aubergine (egg plant) cut side down, until the flesh is soft. Scoop out the flesh and mash. Fry the onion in the same oil, stir in the aubergine (egg plant), breadcrumbs, lemon rind and seasoning, and half the cheese, and the egg. Pile into the aubergine (egg plant) skins. Sprinkle with the rest of the cheese. Place in a well greased oven dish, and bake for 30 minutes in the oven at 375°F, Mark 5.

Vegetables
and salads

In the past, Jewish cuisine was notoriously short of fresh, green vegetables and salads. A gradual change has taken place, and now particularly as a result of the Israeli production and export of countless varieties of vegetables, these play an important part in the Jewish vitamin-conscious diet.

Baked rice and potatoes

4 oz. (⅔ cup) long grained rice
½ teaspoon salt
pinch of pepper
2 tablespoons (2½T) chicken fat
¾ pint (2 cups) chicken stock
½ lb. potatoes
extra salt
serves 3–4

Place the rice in a greased baking dish with the salt, pepper and 1 tablespoon (1¼T) of fat, and stock. Peel and slice the potatoes thinly. Sprinkle them with salt, and place over the rice. Dot with the remaining fat, and cover with foil. Bake in the oven at 375°F, Mark 5, for 1 hour. Remove the foil and bake until brown.

Savoury vegetable strudel

pastry
6 oz. (1½ cups) plain (all purpose) flour
4 oz. (8T) hard margarine, taken from the refrigerator
¼ pint (½ cup+2T) water, approximately
1 teaspoon vinegar

filling
2 tablespoons (2½T) oil or melted margarine
2 onions, chopped
4 oz. mushrooms, sliced
2 tomatoes, skinned and chopped
12 oz. packet frozen spinach
1 tablespoon (1¼T) chopped nuts or sesame seeds
½ teaspoon salt
⅛ teaspoon pepper
pinch of mixed herbs
pinch of garlic salt
1 tablespoon (1¼T) chopped parsley
1½ tablespoons (2¼T) oil or melted margarine for brushing pastry
1 oz. (½ cup) breadcrumbs for sprinkling on pastry
extra nuts or sesame seeds to sprinkle on pastry

Place the flour in a bowl, add the margarine and cut into large pieces. Mix together the water and vinegar and add sufficient to the mixture to make into a soft dough. Roll out the dough into an oblong, fold into three, seal the edges and turn to left. Repeat twice and refrigerate.
Heat the oil. Add the onions and fry until a pale brown. Add the mushrooms, tomatoes and spinach. Add the rest of the filling ingredients and cook for about 10 minutes until the spinach is cooked and liquid evaporated. Leave to cool. Cut the pastry in two, roll out thinly into an oblong, brush with half a tablespoon (¾T) oil, and half the breadcrumbs. Spread half the mixture to within 1 in. of the edge of the pastry. Wet the edges, roll up, brush with the oil and sprinkle with nuts. Repeat with the rest of the pastry and mixture.
Bake in the oven at 425°F, Mark 7, for 20–30 minutes until brown.

Cauliflower latkes

1 cauliflower (2 cups when cooked and pressed down)
1 oz. (2T) matzo meal
2 eggs
salt
pepper
oil for frying
serves 3–4

Cook the cauliflower in boiling, salted water until tender—drain well. Mash the cauliflower, and mix with other ingredients. Fry spoonfuls of the mixture in hot oil on both sides.

Potato latkes

1 lb. potatoes, peeled and
finely grated
1 egg, beaten
1 tablespoon (1¼T) self-raising
flour or matzo meal
salt
pepper
oil for frying
serves 3–4

Squeeze the potatoes until they are dry. Mix in the egg, flour and seasonings.

Heat about ½ in. oil in a frying pan (skillet) and fry spoonfuls of the mixture until they are brown on the underside. Turn and brown on the second side. Drain on absorbent paper. Serve hot with meat or chicken.

Potato pudding Kugel

1 lb. freshly boiled and
mashed potatoes
salt
pepper
2 tablespoons (2½T) chicken fat
or margarine
2 eggs, separated
serves 3–4

Mash the potatoes very well with the seasoning, fat and yolks of egg. Whip the whites of egg very stiffly. Fold into the potato mixture. Pour into a well greased ovenproof dish. Bake in the oven at 425°F, Mark 7, for about 30 minutes.

Grated potato kugel

1 lb. potatoes
salt
pepper
1 tablespoon (1¼T) chicken fat
1 egg
2 tablespoons (2½T) self-raising
flour or matzo meal
serves 3–4

Prepare and grate the potatoes. Drain them well to remove excess moisture. Add the seasoning, fat, beaten egg and the meal, or the flour, mix well. Transfer to a greased pie dish, 1 pint (2½ cups) size. Bake for 45 minutes in the oven at 400°F, Mark 6.

*left: Grated potato kugel; right:
Potato pudding (kugel); top: Kol
bo salad (Everything in salad)*

Potato puffs   Pompishkas

**1 lb. potatoes, steamed in their
jackets, peeled and mashed
1 oz. (2T) margarine
1 egg, separated
salt
pepper
oil for frying**
makes about 3 dozen

Mix the potatoes, margarine, egg yolk and seasoning, and beat well.
Fold in the stiffly beaten egg white. Roll into small balls and fry in
hot oil, or place on greased tin and bake in the oven at 450°F, Mark
8, for 15 minutes until brown. For a firmer pompishka, add 1
tablespoon (1¼T) of matzo meal.
It is best to steam the potatoes as they need to be very dry.

Sweet and sour cabbage

**1 oz. (2T) margarine
1 onion, grated
1 lb. red cabbage, washed and
finely sliced
1 cooking apple, peeled and
chopped
½ teaspoon salt
1 teaspoon sugar, or to taste
1 tablespoon (1¼T) vinegar, or
to taste
2 tablespoons (2½T) water**
serves 4

Melt the fat in a pan and fry the onion gently. Add the cabbage,
apple, salt, sugar, vinegar and water. Transfer to a casserole, cover
tightly and cook for 1 hour in the oven at 375°F, Mark 5.

Savoury rice

**2 tablespoons (2½T) oil
2 onions, chopped
1 green or red pepper, deseeded
and chopped
8 oz. (1⅓ cups) long grained rice
1 pint (2½ cups) stock, or stock
cube dissolved in 1 pint
(2½ cups) water
1 oz. (¼ cup) currants
½ teaspoon salt or to taste
2 oz. (½ cup) peanuts, optional
a few gherkins and strips of red
pepper for garnish**
serves 4

Heat the oil in a pan and fry the chopped onions until pale brown.
Add the chopped peppers, cook for a minute or two, then add the rice
and cook for another minute. Add the stock and bring to the boil;
add the currants, salt and peanuts. Pour into an oven dish and cook
for ¾ hour covered with foil.
Garnish with gherkin 'fans' and strips of pepper.

Carrot tzimmes

**1 lb. carrots
2 oz. (4T) margarine
3 oz. (½ cup) brown sugar
½ pint (1¼ cups) water
¼ teaspoon salt
2 oz. (½ cup) flour blended with
4 tablespoons (5T) cold water**
serves 4

Peel and slice the carrots. Melt the fat in a pan and cook the carrots
until lightly browned. Add the sugar, water and salt, and cook
covered until tender, about 20 minutes. Pour in the blended flour.
Heat 2–3 minutes, to cook flour, stirring all the time.

Carrot tzimmes, using canned carrots

Drain the carrots, reserving the liquid. Fry gently in fat until lightly
brown, add the sugar and liquid from the can and proceed as before.

Einbren of peas and carrots (right)

Pineapple, celery and walnut salad (opposite)

Einbren of peas and carrots

1 oz. (2T) margarine or chicken fat	
pinch of sugar	
1 oz. (¼ cup) flour	
¼ pint (1¼ cups) stock	
1×10 oz. can of carrots	
1×10 oz. can of peas	
seasoning to taste	
serves 6–8	

Melt the fat in a saucepan. Add the sugar and flour and cook until light brown in colour, but not burnt. Remove from the heat, and add the stock a little at a time, beating well. Return to the heat, and bring to the boil. Add the drained vegetables and reheat. Adjust seasoning. Serve hot.
Cooked cabbage can also be served in this sauce.

Honeyed carrots

1 lb. carrots
1 oz. (2T) margarine
½ teaspoon salt
1 tablespoon (1¼T) honey
2 tablespoons (2½T) orange juice
parsley for garnish
serves 4

Peel the carrots and slice very thinly. Place in a greased dish with the rest of the ingredients. Cover closely with foil. Bake in the oven at 375°F, Mark 5, for ¾ hour, or until carrots are tender. Remove the foil and cook until the liquid has almost evaporated.
Sprinkle with finely chopped parsley.
New carrots, if very small, can be left whole.

Pineapple, celery and walnut salad

6 sticks celery, well washed
3 tablespoons (3¾T), canned
pineapple, chopped
1 tablespoon (1¼T) walnuts,
roughly chopped
¼ teaspoon salt
1 teaspoon lemon juice

Slice the celery very finely. Add the other ingredients and mix together lightly.

Orange and chicory salad

1 orange
1 large or 2 small chicory

dressing
1 tablespoon (1¼T) oil
½ teaspoon sugar
¼ teaspoon salt
1 tablespoon (1¼T) lemon juice
chopped parsley, optional
a few black olives for garnish

Peel the orange, removing all the pith. Cut it into very thin slices. Wash the chicory and dry the leaves well. Arrange the chicory and orange slices decoratively on a shallow dish.
Mix very well together the oil, sugar, salt and lemon juice. Pour over the salad. Sprinkle with chopped parsley, and decorate with the olives.

Celery, apple and beetroot salad

4 sticks crisp celery
1 cooking apple
1 medium cooked beetroot
¼ teaspoon salt
1 tablespoon (1¼T) lemon juice

Wash and chop the celery. Peel and chop the apple and beetroot. Mix with the other ingredients.

Potato salad

1½ lb. potatoes (new potatoes if possible)
½ teaspoon salt
3 tablespoons (3¾T) French dressing (see below)
3 tablespoons (3¾T) pickled cucumber and/or olives
2 tablespoons (2½T) chopped spring onions (scallions) or chives
3 tablespoons (3¾T) chopped parsley
mayonnaise and radish roses, black olives for garnish
serves 6

Scrub the potatoes, and boil in their jackets until tender if potatoes are small; if very large, peel and cut up before cooking. Peel and dice the potatoes and add the French dressing while still hot. Add the rest of the ingredients and sufficient mayonnaise to coat the potatoes. Decorate with radish roses and black olives.

French dressing

2 tablespoons (2½T) oil
1 tablespoon (1¼T) vinegar
½ teaspoon salt
pinch of pepper, sugar and mustard

Place all the ingredients in a small screw topped jar and shake well.

Kol bo salad (Everything In salad)

¼ lb. tomatoes, sliced
¼ cucumber, peeled and cubed
1 green or red pepper, sliced
1 stick celery, chopped
a few olives, stoned and chopped
a few spring onions (scallions), chopped, or thin slices of a mild onion
a few gherkins, chopped
2 eggs, hard boiled and quartered
cos (crisp) lettuce coarsely shredded, or chicory

Mix all the ingredients lightly together in a large bowl. Dress with the oil and lemon dressing (below) or with a sour cream dressing just before use.

Dressing

4 tablespoons (5T) olive oil
2 tablespoons (2½T) lemon juice
1 teaspoon salt
¼ teaspoon mustard
⅛ teaspoon garlic powder
1 teaspoon sugar

Place all the ingredients in small screw topped jar and shake well.

Savoury vegetable strudel (left)

left: Orange and chicory salad;
right: Celery, apple and walnut
salad (below)

Kol bo salad with sour cream
(bottom)

Desserts

Known for their sweet tooth, Jews make two sorts of
desserts— 'parve' (containing no milk or meat products)
for concluding any meal, and 'milk' (containing milk or
milk derivatives) to close a menu containing milky dishes.

Apricot squares

5 oz. ($\frac{5}{8}$ cup) margarine
3 oz. ($\frac{3}{8}$ cup) sugar
1 egg
8 oz. (2 cups) self raising flour
1 lb. apricots, washed and stoned (pitted)
1 teaspoon lemon juice

crumble
1½ oz. (3T) margarine
3 oz. ($\frac{3}{4}$ cup) flour
2 oz. ($\frac{1}{4}$ cup) sugar
1 oz. ($\frac{1}{4}$ cup) ground almonds
1 teaspoon sugar, to sprinkle
serves 6

Cream together the margarine and sugar. Add the egg, stirring well. Fold in the flour. Knead well. Press the dough into an 8 in. square tin.
Place the apricots, cut side down, on the dough. Sprinkle with the lemon juice. Place the crumble mixture over the apricots. Sprinkle with 1 teaspoon of sugar. Bake in the oven at 350°F, Mark 4, for 1 hour.

to make crumble: rub the margarine into the flour, and add the sugar and almonds. Mix well.

Fluden

pastry
12 oz. (3 cups) self raising flour
8 oz. (1 cup) margarine
8 oz. (1 cup) sugar
2 eggs
1 tablespoon (1¼T) water
extra sugar

filling
4 oz. (½ cup) apricot jam
4 oz. (1 cup) chopped dates
4 oz. (1 cup) chopped nuts
1 teaspoon cinnamon
1 tablespoon (1¼T) orange juice
mixed together
1 lb. cooking apples, peeled and chopped
2 oz. ($\frac{5}{16}$ cup) brown sugar
juice of 1 lemon
rind of ¼ lemon
extra sugar to sprinkle
serves 10

Place the flour in a bowl, rub in the margarine, add the sugar and make into a dough with 1 egg, 1 yolk of egg and water. Knead well and divide into three, one portion larger than the other two. Roll out the larger piece of dough to fit the bottom and sides of a well greased tin 11 × 7 in. and at least 3 in. deep.
Spread half the jam over the pastry, and sprinkle with the date mixture. Roll out another piece of dough to cover filling. Spread with the rest of the jam. Mix together the apples, sugar and lemon, and place over the jam. Roll out the rest of the pastry to fit over the apples mixture. Beat the remaining egg white. Brush it over the pastry and sprinkle with sugar. Bake in the oven at 350°F, Mark 4, for 30 minutes and then turn down to 325°F, Mark 3, for another 1½ hours. Turn down if fluden is getting too brown.

Apple pie

6 oz. (1½ cups) self raising flour
6 oz. (1½ cups) plain (all purpose) flour
8 oz. (1 cup) margarine
4 oz. (½ cup) sugar
2 eggs
sugar to sprinkle

filling
2 tablespoons (2½T) apricot jam
2 lb. cooking apples
3 oz. ($\frac{3}{8}$ cup) sugar, or to taste
1 oz. ($\frac{1}{4}$ cup) sultanas (white raisins)
juice and rind of lemon
1 teaspoon cinnamon
1 oz. ($\frac{1}{4}$ cup) flour
½ oz. (1T) melted margarine

Mix together the flours and rub in the margarine. Add the sugar. Make into a stiff dough, using 1 egg and 1 yolk, if necessary. Knead lightly, and divide into two, one piece a little larger than the other. Roll out the slightly larger half and line the base and sides of a greased baking tin 9 × 12 × 1 in. deep.
Spread the base with the apricot jam.
Peel, core and slice the apples, mix with the rest of the filling ingredients, and place over pastry. Wet the edges of the pastry. Roll out the rest of pastry and arrange over the apples. Crimp the edges. Brush with the beaten egg white and sprinkle with sugar. Bake in the oven at 425°F, Mark 7, for 20 minutes, reduce the heat to 375°F, Mark 5, and bake until brown for another 20 minutes. Cut into squares to serve.

Apple shalet

1 lb. cooking apples
juice of ½ lemon
3 oz. (1 cup) white breadcrumbs
3 oz. (½ cup) brown sugar
½ teaspoon cinnamon
rind of ½ lemon
2 oz. (4T) margarine
1 tablespoon (1¼T) water
1 red dessert apple
extra lemon juice

serves 2–3

Peel the cooking apples and grate coarsely. Sprinkle with the lemon juice. Mix together the breadcrumbs, sugar, cinnamon and lemon rind.
Grease a pie dish lavishly with some of the margarine.
Put ⅓ of the breadcrumb mixture in the pie dish. Cover with half the apples. Sprinkle with ⅓ of the breadcrumb mixture and dot with half the margarine which is left. Cover with rest of the apples, add the water. Sprinkle with rest of the breadcrumb mixture, and dot with remainder of margarine. Cover with aluminium foil. Bake in the oven at 400°F, Mark 6, for about 45 minutes then remove foil, to brown. Decorate with the thinly sliced dessert apple which has been dipped in lemon juice.
Instead of apples, stoned (pitted) plums, cherries or apricots, gooseberries or rhubarb can be used.

Apple cake

5 oz. (⅝ cup) butter or margarine
3 oz. (⅜ cup) sugar
1 egg
7 oz. (1¾ cups) self raising flour
pinch of salt
1 lb. cooking apples
lemon juice
2 tablespoons (2½T) sugar
2 tablespoons (2½T) apricot jam, optional
icing (confectioner's) sugar

serves 6

Cream together the margarine and sugar, and beat in the egg. Fold in the sifted flour and salt. Spread ¾ of the mixture over the bottom of a greased 7½ in. tin.
Peel, core and slice the apples and squeeze lemon juice over them. Arrange overlapping slices of apple on the mixture in the tin, and sprinkle with the sugar. If wished, brush with the melted apricot jam. Take small pieces of the remaining mixture, roll into strips with floured hands, and arrange in a lattice pattern over apples. Bake for 1 hour in the oven at 325°F, Mark 3.
Dust with icing (confectioner's) sugar while still hot.

note: apricots, cherries, gooseberries or plums may be used instead of apples.
If made with margarine, this dish is parve; if with butter, then it is a milk dessert.

Apple flan

pastry
8 oz. (2 cups) plain (all purpose) flour
pinch of salt
5 oz. (⅝ cup) margarine
2 oz. (⅜ cup) sifted icing (confectioner's) sugar
2 egg yolks

filling
2 tablespoons (2½T) apricot jam
2 tablespoons (2½T) ground almonds, optional
2 lb. cooking apples
3 oz. (⅜ cup) sugar to taste
juice of 1 lemon and grated rind of ¼ lemon
½ teaspoon cinnamon

apricot glaze
1 tablespoon (1¼T) apricot jam
1 dessertspoon water
serves 6

Mix together the flour and salt, rub in the margarine. Add the icing (confectioner's) sugar. Mix to a stiff dough, using as much egg yolk as necessary. Chill if possible.

Roll out the pastry to fit an 8 in. flan dish, press well into the dish. Allow the pastry to rest for a few minutes if possible. Roll a rolling pin over edge of dish to trim off the excess pastry. Prick the pastry and press a sheet of foil firmly on to pastry to help keep its shape. Bake for 10 minutes in the oven at 425°F, Mark 7, and then remove foil and bake for another 5 minutes.

Spread the pastry with jam, and sprinkle with the ground almonds. Peel, core and grate apples, mix with the sugar, lemon rind and juice and cinnamon. Roll out the remaining pastry, and cut into strips. Twist each strip and make lattice pattern over top of the mixture in flan dish. Bake for 10 minutes in the oven at 425°F, Mark 6, then reduce the heat to 350°F, Mark 4, for about 30 minutes, until the apples are soft and the pastry is brown.

to make glaze: boil the water and jam together. Sieve and brush over the pastry.

Bread pudding

4 oz. white bread
1½ oz. (³⁄₁₆ cup) sugar
2 oz. (½ cup) dried fruit
1 egg
1½ oz. (3T) melted margarine
½ oz. (⅛ cup) chopped peel, optional
½ teaspoon mixed spice (allspice)
½ teaspoon cinnamon
½ teaspoon finely grated lemon rind

Soak the bread in cold water and squeeze dry. Mash with a fork. Add all the other ingredients, mix well. Bake in a greased dish for ¾ hour in the oven at 400°F, Mark 6.
Serve with orange sauce.

Orange sauce

1 slightly rounded tablespoon (1¼T) cornflour (cornstarch)
pinch of salt
¼ pint (½ cup+2T) water
¼ pint (½ cup+2T) orange juice
1 teaspoon lemon juice
1 teaspoon finely grated orange rind
½ oz. (1T) margarine
sugar to taste, about 1 tablespoon (1¼T)

Blend together the cornflour (cornstarch), salt and 3 tablespoons (3¾T) water. Bring the rest of the water, juices, rind and margarine to the boil. Pour over the blended cornflour (cornstarch), return to the pan, add the sugar, and cook thoroughly.

Rice kugel

8 oz. (1⅓ cups) rice
2 oz. (8T) margarine, melted
4 oz. (⅝ cup) brown sugar
4 oz. (1 cup) sultanas (white raisins)
1 teaspoon cinnamon
½ teaspoon mixed spice
½ teaspoon grated lemon rind
2 eggs
serves 6

Boil the rice in salted water until just tender. Drain and rinse in cold water. Mix the rice and the other ingredients together. Place in a well greased pie dish—2 pint (5 cups) size. Bake in the oven at 350°F, Mark 4, for 1 hour.

Bread pudding

Lochshen pudding

4 oz. (1½ cups) lochshen
½ teaspoon salt
1½ oz. (³⁄₁₆ cup) sugar
2 oz. (½ cup) sultanas
    (white raisins)
1½ oz. (3T) margarine
1 egg

Bring 2 pints (5 cups) of water to the boil, add the lochshen and salt, and cook for 5 minutes. Drain the lochshen and rinse with cold water. Mix the lochshen, sugar, sultanas (white raisins), melted margarine and beaten egg together. Pour into a greased oven dish— 1½ pint (4 cups). Bake in the oven at 375°F, Mark 5, for 45 minutes. Serve hot with stewed fruit.

variations:

1. Add 1 grated cooking apple to mixture.
2. Add 1 tablespoon (1¼T) red wine and a little grated lemon rind.
3. Add 1 oz. (¼ cup) ground or 1 oz. (¼ cup) chopped almonds.
4. Add 1 teaspoon cinnamon.

serves 3   5. Add 1 oz. (¼ cup) chopped glacé (candied) cherries.

Cherry slices

2½ oz. (5T) margarine
4 oz. (1 cup) self-raising flour
1 oz. (⅛ cup) sugar
1 egg

topping
1 lb. stoned (pitted) cherries
3 oz. (⅜ cup) sugar
1 oz. (¼ cup) flour
½ teaspoon cinnamon
1 oz. (2T) margarine
serves 4—5

Rub the margarine into the flour and add the sugar. Add the egg to form a soft dough. Press the dough into a well-greased 7 in. oven dish. Arrange the cherries all over the top.

Mix together the sugar, flour and cinnamon and sprinkle over cherries. Dot with margarine. Bake in the oven at 350°F, Mark 4, for 1 hour.

Apricots, plums, apples can be used instead of cherries.

Date and honey pudding

2½ oz. (5T) margarine
1½ oz. (4 cups) sugar
1 level tablespoon (1¼T) honey
1 egg
4 oz. (1 cup) self raising flour
1 tablespoon (1¼T) water
1 oz. (¼ cup) chopped dates

Cream the margarine, sugar and honey. Add the egg. Fold in the flour and, if necessary, add the water to make a stiff dropping consistency. Add the dates and mix well. Place in a 5 in. greased pudding basin. Cover with foil and steam for 1½ hours. Serve with honey sauce.

Honey sauce

1 level teaspoon cornflour (cornstarch)
¼ pint (½ cup+2T) water
2 tablespoons (2½T) honey
1 teaspoon lemon juice

serves 4

Mix the cornflour (cornstarch) and 1 tablespoon (1¼T) of the water. Bring the honey, lemon and rest of water, to the boil. Pour over the blended cornflour (cornstarch) and return to the pan, and cook thoroughly.

Fruit ice cream bombe

1 kosher lemon jelly (gelatin mix)
1 medium tin crushed pineapple (13¾ oz.)
1 small, or half a large, parve ice block
½ lb. (2 cups) washed, hulled and sugared strawberries, or other prepared fruit
lady finger biscuits

serves 6–8

Make the jelly using ¼ pint (½ cup + 2T) boiling water. Leave it to cool slightly. Add the crushed pineapple, and the ice cream, cut into slices. Beat together well. Pour the mixture into an 8 in. fluted ring tin, cover with foil and place in the freezer to set.
To remove the mixture from the tin, place the base of the ring tin in a bowl of warm water for a minute, remove the foil and turn upside down onto a cold plate. Fill the centre with the strawberries, reserving a few for decoration. Push the biscuits underneath to form the spokes of a wheel and arrange the strawberries between each biscuit.

Cherry slices (opposite)   *Date and honey pudding (above)*   75

Apricot whip

2 lb. apricots
juice of 1 lemon
sugar to taste
4 egg whites

serves 6

Wash and stone (pit) the apricots and stew in the lemon juice and very little water, just enough to prevent burning; add sugar to taste. Sieve or liquidize.
Fold in the stiffly beaten egg whites.
Serve in individual glasses decorated with angelica.

Parve whip

½ pint (1¼ cups) parve cream
1 tablespoon (1¼T) brandy or
other liqueur
2 lb. (2 cups) fresh fruit, e.g.
strawberries, or well drained
canned fruit

serves 6–8

Whip the parve cream until stiff. Fold in the brandy. Crush the fruit, reserving a few for decoration. Fold the crushed fruit into the parve cream. Serve in individual glasses, decorated with pieces of the whole fruit.

Kissel (below)

top: Pflummen compote, left and right: Parve whip (opposite)

Pflummen compote

8 oz. (1⅓ cups) prunes
¾ pint (2 cups) water
rind of ½ lemon and ½ orange
2 oz. (5/16 cup) brown sugar
or honey, or to taste
1 tablespoon (1¼T)
blanched almonds

serves 4

Soak the prunes overnight in the water with the rinds. Add the sugar or honey. Cover with foil.
Cook until tender in the oven at 350°F, Mark 4, for 1 hour. (They can be stewed gently for 20 minutes.) Remove the peel, add the almonds and serve.

note: all dried fruit including sultanas, apple rings, apricots and pears, or a mixture, can be cooked in this way.

Blintzes

4 oz. (1 cup) plain (all purpose) flour
¼ teaspoon salt
1 egg
½ pint (1¼ cups) milk
1 tablespoon (1¼T) oil
oil for frying
extra butter

serves 3–4

Mix together the flour and salt. Add the egg, milk and oil. Whisk until smooth.

Heat a shallow frying pan (skillet), and add a teaspoon of the oil. Pour in sufficient batter to cover the base of the pan thinly. Fry until brown. Turn the blintzes out on to a plate, add a spoonful of filling and fold up to form a parcel. Repeat until all batter is finished. Place the blintzes in a buttered baking dish, dot with butter and bake in the oven until brown at 375°F, Mark 5, for 30 minutes.

Cheese filling

8 oz. (1⅓ cups) curd cheese
1 egg
2 tablespoons (2½T) sugar, or to taste

Mix all the ingredients together.

variations:

1. Add 1 tablespoon (1¼T) sultanas to the mixture.
2. Place a strawberry or 2–3 stoned (pitted) black cherries in each portion of mixture.

Coconut and raisin filling

4 oz. (1¼ cups) desiccated (dried) coconut
4 oz. (1 cup) raisins
1 tablespoon (1¼T) orange juice
1 teaspoon lemon juice
1 tablespoon (1¼T) sugar
1 small cooking apple, peeled and grated

Mix all the ingredients together.

Cherry filling

1 small can (7½ oz.) black cherries, stoned (pitted)
1 heaped teaspoon cornflour (cornstarch)
1 teaspoon lemon juice

Strain the cherries. Mix together the cornflour (cornstarch) and 2 tablespoons (2½T) juice from the can. Heat the rest of the juice from the can, pour over the blended cornflour (cornstarch). Return to the pan and boil until it thickens. Add the cherries and the lemon juice. Serve with fresh or sour cream.

Cous cous Semolina dessert

1 pint (2½ cups) milk
pinch of salt
2 oz. (⅓ cup) semolina
1 oz. (⅛ cup) sugar
1 oz. (2T) butter
2 oz. (½ cup) chopped or ground almonds
2 oz. (½ cup) dates, chopped
2 oz. (½ cup) raisins
grated rind of ¼ orange and ¼ lemon
whole almonds and cherries for decoration

serves 4

Bring the milk to the boil with the salt. Mix the semolina with the sugar and sprinkle on the milk. Reduce the heat, and cook very gently until the semolina thickens, stirring all the time. Add the rest of the ingredients.

Pour into individual serving dishes and decorate with almonds and cherries.

Serve cold.

Cous cous

Kissel

2½ tablespoons (3¼T) cornflour (cornstarch)
pinch of salt
2 tablespoons (2½T) white wine
1 tablespoon (1¼T) lemon juice
¾ pint (2 cups) fruit purée, sweetened to taste (redcurrants, cherries, strawberries or any other fruit can be used)

Blend together the cornflour (cornstarch), salt, wine and juice. Bring the rest of the purée to the boil and pour over the blended cornflour (cornstarch). Return to the pan and cook, stirring all the time, until thick.
Pour into individual serving dishes, chill, and decorate with cream if liked.

Swetchen plum batter

4 oz. (1 cup) plain (all purpose) flour
pinch of salt
1 egg
½ pint (1¼ cups) milk
1 oz. (2T) butter
½ lb. stoned (pitted) swetchen plums
sugar to sprinkle

Place the flour, salt, egg and milk in a basin, whisk until smooth. Melt the butter in a shallow tin. When the butter is hot arrange the halved stoned plums in the tin, and pour over the batter. Bake in the oven at 425°F, Mark 7, for 30 minutes.
Sprinkle thickly with sugar and serve hot.

Strawberry sour cream dessert

1 large can (15½ oz.) strawberries, or loganberries, fruit cocktail, etc.
1 pint (2½ cups) sour cream
4 oz. (½ cup) sugar
1 heaped teaspoon cornflour (cornstarch)
1 teaspoon lemon juice

serves 6–8

Strain the strawberries, and reserve the juice. Sieve the strawberries to make a purée. Mix together the fruit purée, sour cream and sugar. Place in a well greased 7½ in. loose-bottomed tin and bake for 15 minutes in the oven at 350°F, Mark 4.
Blend the cornflour (cornstarch) with 2 tablespoons (2½T) juice from the can. Bring the rest of the juice to the boil. Pour over the blended cornflour (cornstarch). Return to the pan and cook for 1 minute until thick and clear. Leave to cool, stirring from time to time. When the mixture in the tin is cool, spoon the thickened sauce over the mixture. Refrigerate until you are ready to serve it.

Baklava

pastry
8 oz. (2 cups) plain (all purpose) flour
pinch of salt
6 oz. (¾ cup) hard margarine (from refrigerator)
⅜ pint (1 cup) approximately cold water to mix
1½ teaspoons vinegar

filling
extra butter or margarine
8 oz. (2 cups) finely chopped almonds, walnuts or peanuts
2 oz. (⁵⁄₁₆ cup) brown sugar

syrup
⅛ pint (¼ cup+1T) water
8 oz. (1 cup) sugar
juice of one lemon
extra nuts to sprinkle

For pastry recipe see Vegetable strudel (page 59).
Cut the pastry into four pieces. Roll out each layer to fit a 7 in. square deep baking tin. Place the first layer in the well greased baking tin. Brush with melted butter or margarine. Sprinkle with the nuts mixed with the sugar. Repeat the process to use up the nuts and pastry finishing with a top layer of pastry. Brush the top layer with melted butter and cut into squares or diamond shapes. Bake in the oven at 375°F, Mark 5, for 30 minutes, until the pastry is crisp. Meanwhile boil the water, sugar and lemon juice together until syrupy. Spoon over the baklava while it is still hot. Sprinkle with nuts.

Baklava

Iced almond ring (right)

Continental fruit cake (below)

Yeasty fruit cake (opposite top)

*Cheese chocolate triangle
(opposite below)*

Cakes and biscuits

Symbolic of traditional Jewish hospitality is a piece of cake and a glass of sweet wine. Always great biscuit and cake bakers, Jewish housewives like to have at least one home-made cake at hand for unexpected guests.

Mandelbrot

1 egg
2 oz. (¼ cup) castor (super-fine sugar
3 tablespoons (3¾T) oil
5 oz. (1¼ cups) self raising flour
pinch of salt
2 oz. (1½ cups) chopped, blanched almonds
makes about 12 slices

Whisk the egg, sugar and oil together until thick. Fold in the sifted flour and salt with the almonds. Transfer to a greased loaf tin. Bake for 30 minutes in the oven at 350°F, Mark 4. Allow to cool on a wire rack and then slice. Place the slices on a flat tin and return to the oven for a further 20 minutes.

Cinnamon biscuits

8 oz. (2 cups) self raising flour
4 oz. (½ cup) margarine
4 oz. (⅝ cup) soft brown sugar
¼ teaspoon bicarbonate of soda (baking soda)
½ teaspoon cinnamon
1 teaspoon lemon juice
1 teaspoon orange juice
1 egg, separated
2 tablespoons (2½T) sugar and ½ teaspoon cinnamon mixed
makes about 50 using a 2 in diameter cutter

Place the flour in a bowl, rub in the margarine. Add the sugar, bicarbonate of soda (baking soda), and cinnamon. Add the juices, and the egg yolk and sufficient egg white to form a dough. Roll out half the dough thinly, and cut into rounds. Repeat the process with the rest of the dough. Brush with beaten white of egg. Sprinkle with the cinnamon and sugar mixture. Bake in the oven at 375°F, Mark 5, for 15–20 minutes.

Gevickelte kichlen

4 oz. (1 cup) self-raising flour
4 oz. (1 cup) plain (all purpose) flour
pinch of salt
4 oz. (8T) margarine
4 oz. (½ cup) sugar
1–2 eggs

filling
jam
nuts, chopped
sultanas
peel, chopped
cinnamon
icing (confectioner's) sugar to sprinkle

Sift the flour and salt. Rub in the margarine. Add the sugar and mix into stiff dough with as much of the beaten egg as necessary. Divide the mixture into four, and roll each piece out separately into an oblong. Spread each piece with jam to within ½ in. of the edge. Sprinkle with chopped nuts, sultanas, peel and cinnamon. Wet the edges and roll up. Repeat with the other portions. Bake in the oven on greased tins at 425°F, Mark 7, for 20 minutes.
When cool dust with icing (confectioner's) sugar and cut into slices.

Poppy seed kichlen

5 oz. (⅝ cup) margarine
8 oz. (2 cups) self raising flour
5 oz. (⅝ cup) sugar
1 oz. (¼ cup) poppy seeds
1 egg
makes about 3 dozen

Rub the margarine into the flour. Add the sugar and poppy seeds. Mix in sufficient egg to make a stiff dough. Knead the dough lightly, and roll out half the dough thinly, cut into shapes. Repeat the process with the rest of the dough. Brush with egg.
Bake in the oven at 375°F, Mark 5, for 15–20 minutes.

Kichels

5 oz. (⅝ cup) margarine
8 oz. (2 cups) self raising flour
5 oz. (⅝ cup) sugar
1 egg

makes about 3 dozen

Rub the margarine into the flour. Add the sugar. Stir in sufficient egg to make a stiff dough. Knead lightly, and roll out half the dough thinly. Cut it into shapes. Repeat the process with the rest of the dough. Brush the dough with beaten egg.
Bake in the oven at 375°F, Mark 5, for 15–20 minutes.

In biscuit barrel: Wine biscuits; spilling out of biscuit tin: Nuss kichlen; bottom: Eier kichlen

Spilling out of biscuit tin: Kichels; right: Mandelbrot; bottom: Cinnamon biscuits

Nuss kichlen

4 oz. (8T) margarine
3 oz. (⅜ cup) sugar
yolk of egg
2–3 drops vanilla essence
4 oz. (1 cup) ground hazelnuts
4 oz. (1 cup) plain (all purpose) flour
icing (confectioner's) sugar to sprinkle

makes about 3 dozen

Cream the margarine and sugar together until soft. Beat in the egg and vanilla essence. Fold in the flour and nuts. Roll into small balls, and flatten each with a fork. Bake in the oven for 20 minutes at 350°F, Mark 4. Roll in icing (confectioner's) sugar.

Wine biscuits

5 oz. (⅝ cup) margarine
3 oz. (⅜ cup) sugar
1 egg
2 teaspoons wine
10 oz. (2½ cups) self-raising flour
jam
extra sugar to sprinkle

makes about 4 dozen

Cream together the margarine and sugar. Beat in the egg and wine. Fold in the flour.
Form into small balls, make a depression in the middle of each with the floured handle of a wooden spoon. Place a little jam in the middle of each biscuit. Sprinkle with sugar.
Place on a greased tin, bake in the oven at 375°F, Mark 5, for 15–20 minutes.

Eier kichlach

3 eggs
4 tablespoons (5T) oil
2 tablespoons (2½T) sugar
¼ teaspoon salt
4 oz. (1 cup) plain (all purpose) flour

Beat the eggs well. Beat in the oil. Beat in the sugar, salt and flour. Drop teaspoons of the mixture on to a greased baking sheet, well apart. Bake in the oven at 325°F, Mark 3, for 15–20 minutes until brown and puffy.

Schwarzwalde

Kipfel

8 oz. (1 cup) butter or margarine
3 oz. (⅜ cup) sugar
2 teaspoons hot water
2–3 drops vanilla
essence (extract)
12 oz. (3 cups) plain (all
purpose) flour
2 oz. (½ cup) chopped nuts
icing (confectioner's) sugar which
has had a vanilla bean standing in
the packet for some days before

makes 5 dozen

Cream together the margarine and sugar. Add the water and essence. Add the flour and nuts, and mix well. Chill in the refrigerator overnight, if possible.

With floured hands, form the mixture into small rolls about 3 in. long and pencil-sized. Place in crescent shapes on greased tins. Bake in the oven at 400°F, Mark 6, for 15 minutes. Roll in the icing (confectioner's) sugar.

Continental fruit slices

5 oz. (⅝ cup) margarine
3 oz. (⅜ cup) sugar
1 egg
7 oz. (1¾ cups) self-raising flour

filling
1 cooking apple, peeled
4 oz. (1 cup) sultanas
(white raisins)
4 oz. (1 cup) raisins
2 oz. (½ cup) currants
2 oz. (¼ cup) sugar
1 teaspoon cinnamon
juice of 1 lemon

Cream together the margarine and sugar. Beat in the egg. Fold in the flour.

Press three quarters of the mixture into a greased 7 in. square tin. Spread with the filling. Dip your fingers in flour, and taking small pieces of the remaining dough, roll it into strips and place in lattice work over the filling. Bake in the oven at 325°F, Mark 3, for 1 hour.

filling: mince together the apple and dried fruit, add the sugar, cinnamon and lemon juice and then mix well.

Almond biscuits

5 oz. ($\frac{5}{8}$ cup) margarine
5 oz. ($\frac{5}{8}$ cup) sugar
1 egg
few drops almond essence
8 oz. (2 cups) plain (all purpose) flour
3 oz. ($\frac{3}{4}$ cup) ground almonds
2 tablespoons (2$\frac{1}{2}$T) sugar and 2 tablespoons (2$\frac{1}{2}$T) chopped almonds
blanched almonds for decoration
makes about 50

Cream together the margarine and sugar. Add 1 egg and the essence. Mix in the flour and almonds to form a dough. Roll into small balls. Roll the balls in the almond and sugar mixture. Press flat and decorate each with an almond. Place on a greased tin, and bake in the oven at 400°F, Mark 6, for 15–20 minutes.

Almond biscuits

Walnut and cherry squares

dough for continental fruit slices, see page 88
4 oz. ($\frac{1}{2}$ cup) glacé (candied) cherries, chopped
2 oz. ($\frac{1}{2}$ cup) walnuts, chopped
sugar to sprinkle

Mix the cherries and walnuts into the dough. Spread dough into a greased 7 in. square tin. Sprinkle with sugar. Bake in the oven at 325°F, Mark 3, for 1 hour.

Hazelnut bars

pastry
4 oz. (8T) margarine
6 oz. (1$\frac{1}{2}$ cups) plain (all purpose) flour
2 tablespoons (2$\frac{1}{2}$T) water
3 tablespoons (3$\frac{3}{4}$T) apricot jam

filling
4 oz. (8T) margarine
6 oz. ($\frac{3}{4}$ cup) castor (super-fine) sugar
few drops vanilla essence
$\frac{1}{2}$ teaspoon lemon juice
2 eggs
2 oz. ($\frac{1}{4}$ cup) self-raising flour
8 oz. (2 cups) ground hazelnuts
icing (confectioner's) sugar to sprinkle

To make the pastry, rub the margarine into the flour, and make it into a stiff dough with the water. Roll the pastry out to fit an 8 × 12 in. tin. Line the tin with the pastry, prick well and bake in the oven at 425°F, Mark 7, for 10 minutes. Remove from the oven and spread with jam.

filling: cream together the margarine and sugar with the vanilla essence and lemon juice. Beat in the eggs. Add the flour and nuts and mix well. Spread the mixture over the jammed pastry and bake in the oven at 350°F, Mark 4, for 30–40 minutes. Sprinkle with sifted icing (confectioner's) sugar and cut into bars to serve.

overleaf: Schnecken (top left)   *Apple strudel (bottom left)*   *Pineapple cheese cake (right)*

Cheese buns

½ oz. (½ cake compressed) yeast,
or ¼ oz. (2 teaspoons)
dried yeast
about ⅛ pint (¼ cup+1T)
warm water
1 oz. (⅛ cup) sugar
8 oz. (2 cups) plain (all
purpose) flour
¼ teaspoon salt
6 oz. (¾ cup) margarine
1 egg

filling
1 lb. (2⅔ cups) curd cheese
1 egg
2 oz. (¼ cup) sugar
2 oz. (½ cup) sultanas (white
raisins), optional

glacé icing
8 oz. (1½ cups) of sifted icing
(confectioner's) sugar
2 teaspoons lemon juice

Mix the yeast with 2 tablespoons (2½T) warm water and 1 teaspoon sugar and leave for 5–10 minutes in a warm place until bubbly. Mix together the flour, salt, and the rest of the sugar. Rub in 1 oz. (2T) of margarine. Make a hollow in the centre of the mixture, add the egg, yeast mixture and enough warm water to make a soft dough. Beat well. Turn on to a board and knead until smooth. Roll into an oblong, and cover two-thirds of the oblong with one-third of remaining margarine which has been cut into small pieces. Fold the lower edge up one-third, bring the top edge down to meet it, and seal edges. Turn to the left and repeat the process twice with the rest of margarine, and once without. Chill well.
Beat together all ingredients for filling until smooth.
Roll out the pastry thinly, and cut into 2 in. squares. Place teaspoonfuls of the cheese mixture in the middle. Damp the edges. Fold each corner to the centre, and place on a greased tin a little apart. Allow to rise in cool place until puffy. Bake in the oven at 450°F, Mark 8, for 15 minutes.
For glacé icing, mix sugar and lemon juice together with enough water to make into a coating consistency. Spread with glacé icing while still warm.

Jam buns

cheese bun pastry, see above

Roll out the pastry thinly and cut into squares. Place a teaspoon of jam in the centre of each square. Wet edges. Allow the dough to rise, bake and ice as for cheese buns.

Fruity buns

cheese bun pastry, see above
filling
margarine
sultanas (white raisins) or other
dried fruit
sugar
cinnamon
chopped almonds

Roll out the pastry into a square. Brush with melted margarine. Sprinkle with the dried fruit, sugar and cinnamon. Wet the edges and roll up tightly. Cut into slices, and place cut side down on greased tin a little apart. Allow the dough to rise, then bake in the oven at 450°F, Mark 8, for 15 minutes. Ice as for cheese buns and then sprinkle with the chopped almonds.

Pineapple triangles

cheese bun pastry, see above
canned pineapple chunks,
(or apricots, or sugared slices
of raw apples)

Roll out the pastry thinly, and cut into squares. Place the pineapple chunks in the centre of each square. Wet the edges, and fold in triangles. Allow the dough to rise, bake as for cheese buns, see above.

Iced almond ring

half the cheese bun pastry
4 oz. (1 cup) ground almonds
4 oz. (½ cup) sugar
1 teaspoon lemon juice
yolk of egg
2 tablespoons (2½T) jam
glacé icing made from 4 oz.
(¾ cup) icing
(confectioner's) sugar
blanched almonds and glacé
(candied) cherries and angelica
[candied peel] to decorate

Mix together the almonds, sugar, lemon juice and yolk of egg. Roll out the pastry into a square. Spread with jam, and then spread with the almond mixture. Wet the edges.
Roll up and arrange as a circle on a greased tin, or in an 8 in. greased ring tin. Allow to rise in cool place until puffy. Bake in the oven at 450°F, Mark 8, for 25 minutes. When cold, ice with glacé icing, and decorate with the blanched almonds, glacé (candied) cherries, and angelica.

Stuffed monkey

**6 oz. (1½ cups) plain (all
purpose) flour
½ teaspoon cinnamon
4 oz. (8T) margarine
4 oz. (⅝ cup) soft brown sugar
1 egg
flaked almonds for sprinkling**

**filling
1½ oz. (3T) margarine
2 oz. (⅓ cup) chopped peel
(candied peel)
2 oz. (⅓ cup) chopped almonds
2 oz. (⅓ cup) sultanas
(white raisins)
1 oz. (⅛ cup) sugar
yolk of egg
a few drops almond essence
½ teaspoon cinnamon
½ teaspoon mixed spice (allspice)**

Sift the flour and cinnamon. Rub in the margarine. Add the sugar
and make into a soft dough with the beaten egg (leave a little white
for brushing). Knead and divide into two. Roll out one piece to fit a
greased 7 in. square tin.
Make the filling by melting the margarine and adding the other
ingredients. Spread the filling on the pastry. Cover with the rest of
the pastry, and seal edges. Brush with the beaten egg white and
sprinkle with almonds. Bake in the oven at 375°F, Mark 5, for 30
minutes.
Cut into squares to serve.

Almond slices

**4 oz. (8T) margarine
6 oz. (1½ cups) plain (all
purpose) flour
1 oz. (1 cup) sugar
1 egg yolk
2 tablespoons (2½T) jam**

**filling
4 oz. (8T) margarine
4 oz. (½ cup) sugar
2 eggs
2–3 drops almond essence
4 oz. (1 cup) ground almonds
2 oz. (⅓ cup) semolina
flaked almonds for decoration**

Rub the margarine into the flour. Add the sugar and egg to make a
stiff dough. Knead the dough lightly and roll out to line a greased tin
11 × 8 in. Prick the pastry with a fork. Bake for 10 minutes in the
oven at 425°F, Mark 7. Remove from the oven and spread with the
jam.

filling: cream together the margarine and sugar. Gradually beat in
the eggs mixed with the essence. Fold in the almonds and semolina.
Spread over the pastry. Sprinkle with the flaked almonds. Bake in the
oven at 350°F, Mark 4, for about 45 minutes until brown.
Cut into bars to serve.

93

Marble angel cake

4 oz. (8T) margarine
4 oz. (½ cup) sugar
1 teaspoon vanilla sugar or
2 drops vanilla essence
2 eggs
5 oz. (1¼ cups) self raising flour
2 tablespoons (2½T) warm water
1 tablespoon (1¼T) cocoa
icing (confectioner's) sugar
to sprinkle

Cream together the margarine and sugar with the vanilla. Add the beaten eggs, a little at a time. Fold in the sifted flour alternately with the water.

Put half the mixture into a separate bowl. Add the sifted cocoa to one half of the mixture. Place alternate spoonfuls into a well greased 7½ in. angel cake tin. Bake in the oven at 350°F, Mark 4, for 40 minutes. When cool sprinkle with sifted icing (confectioner's) sugar.

Kiddush sultana cake

5 oz. (⅝ cup) margarine
5 oz. (⅝ cup) castor (superfine) sugar
1 teaspoon vanilla sugar, or 2 drops vanilla essence
¼ teaspoon grated lemon rind
2 eggs
8 oz. (2 cups) self raising flour
4 tablespoons (5T) warm water
4 oz. (1 cup) sultanas (white raisins)
1 tablespoon (1¼T) flaked almonds

Cream together the margarine and sugar with the vanilla essence and lemon rind. Add the beaten eggs, and fold in the flour alternately with the water. Fold in the fruit. Place in a well greased tin 7½ × 11 in. and 1½ in. deep. Sprinkle with the flaked almonds. Bake in the oven at 350°F, Mark 4, for ¾ hour.

variations: 4 oz. (1 cup) mixed currants, sultanas (white raisins), raisins, chopped peel and glacé (candied) cherries.

Barmitzvah cake

8 oz. (1 cup) margarine
8 oz. (1 cup) castor (superfine)
sugar, or 8 oz. (1¼ cups) soft
brown sugar
pinch of salt
grated rind of ½ lemon and
½ orange
½ teaspoon vanilla essence
½ teaspoon almond essence
½ level teaspoon cinnamon
½ level teaspoon mixed spices
pinch of nutmeg
5 eggs
9 oz. (2¼ cups) plain (all
purpose) flour
9 oz. (2¼ cups) sultanas
(white raisins)
6 oz. (1½ cups) currants
5 oz. (1¼ cups) raisins
3 oz. (¾ cup) chopped or
ground almonds
4 oz. (½ cup) glacé
(candied) cherries
3 oz. (¾ cup) (candied) peel
pinch of bicarbonate of soda
(baking soda) in
1 teaspoon brandy

Cream together the margarine and sugar and all the flavourings. Add the beaten eggs, a little at a time. Add the sifted flour. Add the fruit, almonds and the cherries (cut into four and floured). Add the bicarbonate of soda (baking soda) and brandy, mix well. Turn into a prepared tin, smooth the top, and tie the brown paper round the outside of the tin. Bake in the middle of the oven at 300°F, Mark 2, for about 4 hours.

Cool thoroughly. Store in a tin. The can can be covered with almond paste and royal icing.

to prepare tin: grease an 8 in. diameter tin or a 7 in. square. Completely line it with greased greaseproof paper, by cutting a slip of paper 3 in. wider than the depth of the tin and 1 in. longer than the circumference. Fold up 1 in. and slash diagonally with scissors. Line the tin and cut a circle to fit the base. Tie a double sheet of brown paper around the tin and stand the tin on a baking sheet.

Almond paste

1 lb. (4 cups) ground almonds
8 oz. (1 cup) castor
(superfine) sugar
8 oz. (1½ cups) icing
(confectioner's) sugar, sifted
2 teaspoons lemon juice
¼ teaspoon vanilla essence
2 drops almond essence
2 eggs
sieved apricot jam

Mix together the ground almonds and sugars, add the juice, essences and sufficient egg to make into a soft paste. Knead the paste until smooth. Brush the bottom and sides of cake with apricot jam (bottom of the cake is smoother than top). Roll out half the paste to form a round, and place on the cake. Roll out the rest of the paste to form a strip to fit the sides. Place the cake on its side on the almond paste and roll the paste round the cake, pressing the paste down and pressing the ends to join evenly. Turn right side up and use rolling pin to make the top flat and the sides flat. Leave at least 1 day to dry out before icing.

Royal icing

1 lb (3 cups) icing
(confectioner's) sugar, sifted
2 egg whites
1 teaspoon lemon juice

Add the egg whites and lemon juice to the sugar and beat very well until it is smooth. With a palette knife, dipped in hot water, spread the icing smoothly all over the cake. Leave 1 day at least, before adding decorations.

Plan the decorations on paper first.
Make up ½ lb (1½ cups) royal icing.
Colour a little with a few drops of blue colouring, and pipe on decorations.

Lebskuchen

2 eggs
2 oz. (¼ cup) granulated sugar
4 oz. (⅝ cup) brown sugar
2 tablespoons (2½T) grated chocolate
1 level tablespoon (1¼T) honey
grated rind of ½ lemon and ½ orange
few drops vanilla essence
1 oz. (¼ cup) nuts, chopped
4 oz. (1 cup) plain (all purpose) flour
½ level teaspoon baking powder
½ level teaspoon mixed spice (allspice)

icing
4 oz. (¾ cup) icing (confectioner's) sugar
enough water to make a thin coating

Beat together the eggs and sugar until creamy. Beat in the chocolate, honey, grated rinds, essence, and nuts. Fold in the sifted flour, baking powder and spice. Spread in shallow greased tin 12 × 9 in. Bake in the oven at 350°F, Mark 4, for 30 minutes. Spread with glacé icing while warm, and cut into squares.

Kiddush chocolate cake

Kiddush chocolate cake

4 oz. (8T) soft margarine
4 oz. (½ cup) sugar
1 teaspoon vanilla sugar or 2 drops vanilla essence
5 oz. (1¼ cups) self raising flour and 1 level teaspoon baking powder sieved together
2 oz. (½ cup) cocoa
2 eggs
3 tablespoons (3¾T) hot water

Place all the ingredients in a large mixing bowl and beat until creamy. Place in a well greased tin 7 × 7 × 1 in. Bake in the oven at 350°F, Mark 4, for ¾ hour.

Yeasty fruit cake

1 oz. fresh yeast (1 cake compressed yeast) or ½ oz. (4 teaspoons) dried yeast
1 teaspoon sugar
1 tablespoon (1¼T) warm water
8 oz. (1 cup) margarine
8 oz. (1 cup) sugar
3 eggs
12 oz. (3 cups) plain (all purpose) flour
4 oz. (1 cup) sultanas (white raisins) and raisins, mixed
2½ oz. (⅝ cup) mixed chopped crystallised (candied) pineapple, and glacé (candied) cherries and orange and lemon (candied) peel

Mix together the yeast, sugar and warm water and leave in a warm place until bubbly. Cream together the margarine and sugar. Add the eggs, a little at a time. Add the flour, fruit and yeast mixture, mix well. Pour into a greased tin 7½ × 11 in. Place in a greased polythene bag, leave to rise in warm place until puffy. Bake in the oven at 350°F, Mark 4, for 1 hour.

Schnecken

½ oz. (½ cake compressed yeast)
yeast or ¼ oz. (2 teaspoons)
dried yeast
1 teaspoon sugar
1 tablespoon (1¼T) warm water
8 oz. (2 cups) plain (all purpose)
flour (strong if possible)
½ teaspoon salt
1 oz. (2T) margarine or butter
1 oz. (1 cup) sugar
1 egg
warm water to mix, about 2–3
tablespoons (2½T–3¾T)

filling
1 oz. (2T) melted margarine
2 oz. (½ cup) sultanas
(white raisins)
1 oz. (¼ cup) chopped nuts
1 teaspoon cinnamon
1 oz. (1¼T) brown sugar

to coat tin
extra butter or margarine,
about 1 oz. (2T)
extra brown sugar (1½
tablespoons (2T))
2 tablespoons (2½T) water

glaze
1 tablespoon (1¼T) sugar
dissolved in a little
boiling water
extra sugar
makes 12

Mix the yeast with a teaspoon of sugar and a tablespoon of warm water and leave in warm place until bubbly. Mix together the flour and salt, and rub in the margarine; add the sugar. Pour the yeast mixture into the centre of the flour mixture. Add the egg and enough warm water to make a stiff dough. Beat well, and turn on to a floured board and knead well.

Roll out into a square. Brush with the melted margarine, and sprinkle with the rest of the filling ingredients. Wet the edges and roll up tightly. Brush with the rest of the margarine. Cut into 1 in. slices. Grease a deep tin very lavishly with butter or margarine, sprinkle thickly with the brown sugar, and then sprinkle with a little water. Place the slices in the tin, and slip into a greased polythene bag. Leave in a warm place until double in size.

Bake in the oven at 425°F, Mark 6, for about 20–30 minutes. Leave to cool for a little. Brush with the glaze and sprinkle with sugar.

Chocolate roll

half the dough
2 oz. (4T) margarine
2 tablespoons (2½T) cocoa
2 oz. ($\frac{5}{16}$ cup) brown sugar
few drops vanilla essence

Melt the margarine in a saucepan. Add the cocoa and sugar. Bring to the boil and add the essence. Cool.

Roll out the dough to form an oblong, the length of the baking tin. Spread with the filling to within 1 in. of the edge. Damp the edges and roll up tightly. Place on a greased tin, and brush the roll with water. Place the tin in a greased polythene bag. Leave to rise in a warm place until double the size. Bake in the oven at 400°F, Mark 6, for 30 minutes. Brush with the sugar water.

sugar water: place a tablespoon (1¼T) water in a saucepan. Add 1 tablespoon (1¼T) sugar. Heat to dissolve the sugar.

Fruit roll

Brush the pastry with margarine, sprinkle with sultanas (white raisins), sugar and cinnamon. Proceed as for chocolate roll.

Kugelhof

½ oz. fresh yeast (½ cake compressed yeast) or ¼ oz. (2 teaspoons) dried yeast
1 tablespoon (1¼T) warm water
1 teaspoon sugar
6 oz. (1¼ cups) plain (all purpose) flour
½ teaspoon salt
2 oz. (4T) margarine
1 oz. (1 cup) sugar
1 egg
¼ pint (½ cup+2T) warm milk
2 oz. (½ cup) sultanas (white raisins), if liked
halved almonds, if liked
icing (confectioners') sugar for decoration

Mix together the yeast and water with a teaspoon of sugar, and leave for 5–10 minutes until bubbly. Sift the flour and salt, and rub in the margarine. Add the sugar. Add the egg, yeast mixture and milk. Beat for 5 minutes. Add the sultanas (white raisins), if used.

Grease an 8 in. Kugelhof pan or tube tin very well. Decorate the bottom with blanched almonds, if used. Half fill the tin with the mixture. Slip into a plastic bag. Leave in a warm place until doubled in size. Bake in the oven at 375°F, Mark 5, for 45 minutes. Turn out and dust with icing (confectioner's) sugar. Use the same day.

Kugelhof

Nusskuchen

6 oz. (¾ cup) sugar
4 eggs
few drops vanilla essence
4 oz. (1 cup) self raising flour
4 oz. (1 cup) hazelnuts,
chopped finely

icing
4 oz. (¾ cup) icing
(confectioner's) sugar
2 teaspoons lemon juice
water

Warm the bowl. Add the sugar, eggs and vanilla essence, and whisk until very thick. Fold in the sieved flour and nuts. Bake in a greased 8 in. sponge tin, in the oven at 350°F, Mark 4, for 1 hour.
Sift the icing (confectioner's) sugar. Add the lemon juice and sufficient water to make into a thick cream. Spread over the cake and leave to set.

Chocolate nusskuchen

4 oz. (8T) margarine
4 oz. (½ cup) sugar
2 eggs
2 oz. (½ cup) self raising flour
2 oz. (½ cup) ground hazelnuts,
slightly roasted
1 oz. (1 square) grated chocolate
icing (confectioners') sugar
to sprinkle

butter cream
2 oz. (4T) margarine
4 oz. (¾ cup) icing
(confectioners') sugar
1 teaspoon instant coffee,
dissolved in 2 teaspoons
boiling water

Cream together the margarine and sugar. Beat in the eggs. Fold in the flour, nuts and chocolate. Place in two greased 6 in. sandwich tins. Bake in the oven at 350°F, Mark 4, for 25–30 minutes.
Cream all the ingredients for butter cream together very well. Sandwich together with butter cream when cool. Dust with the sifted icing (confectioner's) sugar.

Purim kalisch

1 oz. fresh yeast (1 cake
compressed yeast), or ½ oz.
(4 teaspoons) dried yeast
1 tablespoon (1¼T) warm water
1 teaspoon sugar
1 lb. (4 cups) plain (all purpose)
strong flour
1 teaspoon salt
2 oz. (¼ cup) sugar
2 oz. (¼ cup) margarine
2 eggs
warm water to mix

glacé icing
4 tablespoons (5T) icing
(confectioners') sugar, and
water to make a thin paste
coloured strands
(see illustration)

Mix together the yeast, water and 1 teaspoon sugar, leave until bubbly. Mix together the flour, salt and sugar. Rub in the margarine. Mix the eggs with the yeast mixture. Pour this mixture into the centre of the flour and using warm water, if necessary, make into a stiff dough. Beat well. Knead on a board until smooth.
Divide into four pieces. Knead each, and roll into long strips and plait together. Or, alternatively, divide into two pieces, rolling each into a strip about 14 in. long. Place across one another on a board. Then take the two opposite ends of each strip, cross them over in centre. Cross each strip alternately three times. Gather short ends together and lay the plait on its side. Brush with water. Place on a greased tin, and slip into a greased polythene bag. Leave in a warm place until doubled in size. Bake in the oven at 400°F, Mark 6, for about 30–40 minutes, until loaf sounds hollow when tapped. Brush with thin glacé icing and sprinkle with coloured strands (see illustration).

Kuchen

1 oz. fresh yeast ($\frac{1}{2}$ cake
compressed yeast) or $\frac{1}{2}$ oz.
(4 teaspoons) dried yeast
1 teaspoon sugar
2 tablespoons (2$\frac{1}{2}$T) warm water
1 lb. (4 cups) plain (all
purpose) flour
$\frac{1}{2}$ teaspoon salt
4 oz. (8T) margarine
4 oz. ($\frac{1}{2}$ cup) sugar
2–4 oz. ($\frac{1}{2}$–1 cup) sultanas
(white raisins), if liked
2 eggs
warm water

crumble
3 oz. ($\frac{3}{4}$ cup) flour
2 oz. (4T) margarine
2 oz. ($\frac{1}{4}$ cup) sugar
$\frac{1}{2}$ teaspoon cinnamon

Mix the yeast with 1 teaspoon of sugar and water, leave for 5–10 minutes until bubbly. Mix together the flour and salt. Rub in the margarine and add the sugar and fruit. Pour the yeast mixture and eggs into a well in the centre of the flour. Using water, gradually mix to form a stiff dough. Beat well. Turn on to a board and knead well. Roll lightly to the shape of a 12 × 9 in. tin, or two small tins. Place in a greased tin, brush with water and place in a greased polythene bag. Leave in a warm place to rise until double the size. This will take 1$\frac{1}{2}$ hours in a warm place but can be left in a cooler place for a longer time.

to make crumble: sift the flour. Rub in the margarine. Add the sugar and cinnamon.
Sprinkle with crumble mixture and bake in the oven at 400°F, Mark 6, for 1 hour, or 45 minutes if 2 tins are used.

Almond cake

**6 oz. ($\frac{3}{4}$ cup) margarine
or butter
6 oz. ($\frac{3}{4}$ cup) castor
(superfine) sugar
3 eggs
3 drops almond essence
6 oz. ($1\frac{1}{2}$ cups) self raising flour
3 oz. ($\frac{3}{4}$ cup) ground almonds
1 tablespoon ($1\frac{1}{4}$T) water
$\frac{1}{2}$ oz. (1 cup) flaked almonds**

Cream together the margarine and sugar. Beat in the eggs, one at a time with the almond essence. Fold in the sifted flour and ground almonds and water. Place in a 7 in. square tin lined with greased greaseproof paper. Sprinkle with the flaked almonds. Bake in the oven at 325°F, Mark 3, for $1\frac{1}{4}$ hours.

Almond cake

Schwarzwalde

Chocolate cream layer cake

**3 eggs
pinch of salt
$2\frac{1}{2}$ oz. ($\frac{5}{16}$ cup) castor
(superfine) sugar
$\frac{1}{2}$ oz. ($\frac{1}{8}$ cup) cocoa
$1\frac{1}{2}$ oz. ($\frac{3}{8}$ cup) self raising flour
1 tablespoon ($1\frac{1}{4}$T) rum
or brandy**

**filling
$\frac{1}{2}$ pint (2 cups) cream, whipped
1 egg white, stiffly beaten
chocolate finely grated
chocolate flakes grated on a
vegetable peeler
icing (confectioners') sugar
to sprinkle**

Whip the egg whites with salt until very stiff. Whip in the sugar. Whip in the egg yolks. Gently fold in the sifted cocoa and flour. Bake in three 5 in. greased sandwich tins, in the oven at 400°F, Mark 6, for 12–15 minutes. Sprinkle the rum or brandy over the cooked cakes. When cold sandwich them together with the whipped cream, into which a stiffly beaten egg white is folded. Spread the whipped cream over the sides of the cake and roll in the grated chocolate. Cover top with the rest of the cream and sprinkle with chocolate flakes grated on a vegetable peeler. Sift the icing (confectioner's) sugar over top. Doubling the quantity makes two $9\frac{1}{2}$ in. tins which can be split to make four layers.

Sultana and nut rugelach

**4 oz. (8T) margarine
4 oz. (1 cup) plain (all
purpose) flour
4 oz. ($\frac{2}{3}$ cup) curd cheese
icing (confectioners') sugar
to sprinkle**

**filling
1 oz. ($\frac{1}{4}$ cup) sultanas
(white raisins)
1 tablespoon ($1\frac{1}{4}$T) sugar
$\frac{1}{4}$ teaspoon cinnamon, if liked**

makes about 2 dozen

Rub the margarine into the flour. Add the curd cheese and mix well to form dough. Chill.
Roll out half the pastry and cut into triangles. Brush the top of the pastry with water. Place a small part of the filling in the centre of each triangle. Roll up from wide side. Place on a greased tin. Bake in the oven at 425°F, Mark 7, for 15 minutes. Sprinkle with icing (confectioner's) sugar.
The pastry can be rolled into an oblong and spread with filling, then rolled up tightly, and cut into slices. The slices are placed cut side down on a greased tin.

Cheese chocolate triangle

4 oz. (8T) margarine or butter
4 oz. (½ cup) sugar
1 lb. (2⅔ cups) curd cheese
grated rind of ¼ lemon (optional)
1 egg
few drops vanilla essence
2 packets Petite Beurre
(36 biscuits)
milk

chocolate coating
4 oz. (½ cup) sugar
3 tablespoons (3¾T) cocoa
2 tablespoons (2½T) water
1 teaspoon coffee
3 oz. (⅜ cup) margarine

Cream together the sugar and margarine. Add the cheese, grated lemon rind, egg and vanilla essence and beat well until smooth. Dip the Petite Beurre biscuits in milk and arrange four rows of three biscuits on a sheet of foil. Spread a layer of the cheese mixture on top. Repeat twice more. Cover with the rest of the cheese mixture, and pile up in centre. Put your hands underneath the foil and bring the outer row of biscuits to meet in the centre, forming a triangle. Leave in the refrigerator while making the coating.
Put the cocoa, sugar, water and coffee in pan and boil until thick. Remove and add the margarine cut in pieces, beat well. When cool pour over the top of the cake and leave to set overnight in the refrigerator.

Pineapple cheese cake

biscuit base
6 oz. (about 18) crushed
digestive biscuits
(graham crackers)
2 oz. (4T) melted butter

filling
8 oz. (1 cup) cream cheese
2 eggs
4 oz. (½ cup) sugar
2–3 drops vanilla essence
small can (8½ oz. size) pineapple
cubes, chopped or pieces

topping
¼ pint (½ cup) sour cream
pieces of pineapple, glacé
(candied) cherries, angelica
(candied peel) and thin squares
of chocolate for decorations

Mix together the biscuits and melted butter. Place in foil lined, loose bottomed 7 in. square cake tin.
Mix together the cream cheese, eggs, sugar and vanilla essence, very well. Fold in the well drained pineapple. Pour the mixture over the biscuit base. Bake in the oven at 375°F, Mark 5, for 1 hour. When cool pour the sour cream over the cake. Refrigerate until required. Decorate with the pineapple, glacé (candied) cherries, angelica and chocolate.

Cheese torte

4 oz. (8T) margarine
6 oz. (1½ cups) plain (all
purpose) flour
2 tablespoons (2½T) water

filling
2 oz. (4T) margarine
2 oz. (¼ cup) sugar
1 egg
½ lb. (1⅓ cup) curd cheese
2 tablespoons (2½T) single
(light) cream, or
top-of-the-milk
2–3 drops vanilla essence
½ teaspoon lemon juice
milk or egg for glaze

Rub the margarine into the flour, and mix to a dough with water. Knead lightly, and roll out to fit a greased 7½ in. flan dish. Press a sheet of foil firmly over pastry. Bake in the oven at 425°F, Mark 7, for 10 minutes. Remove the foil and bake for a further 5 minutes.
Cream together the margarine and sugar. Add the eggs and beat well. Beat in rest of the ingredients. Pour into the baked pastry case. Cut left over pastry into strips, and make into lattice pattern over cheese filling. Brush the pastry with a little egg or milk. Bake in the oven at 350°F, Mark 4, for 30 minutes.

Jam turnovers

4 oz. (8T) margarine
4 oz. (1 cup) plain (all purpose) flour
4 oz. (1 cup) cooking cheese, grated
jam
icing (confectioners') sugar to sprinkle
makes about 2 dozen

Rub the margarine into the flour. Add the cheese and mix well to form a dough. Chill.
Roll out the pastry, and cut into rounds. Damp the edges. Put a little jam on each round. Fold over and seal well. Place on a greased tin. Bake in the oven at 425°F, Mark 7, for 15 minutes. Sprinkle with icing (confectioner's) sugar.

Apple strudel

6 oz. (1½ cups) plain (all purpose) flour, strong flour if possible
pinch of salt
1 tablespoon oil
1 egg
4 tablespoons (5T) warm water
4 tablespoons (5T) oil, approximately to glaze pastry
icing (confectioners') sugar to sprinkle

filling
2 oz. (1 cup) breadcrumbs
2 oz. (½ cup) sultanas (white raisins)
1 lb. cooking apples, chopped
2 oz. (¼ cup) sugar, or to taste
grated rind and juice of ½ lemon
1 teaspoon cinnamon

Mix together the flour and salt. Add the oil, egg and water to make soft dough. Knead well until smooth. Leave covered by warm bowl for 30 minutes. Roll out half the pastry at a time on a floured sheet of greaseproof paper. Roll until paper thin. Brush with oil, and sprinkle with breadcrumbs. Mix the rest of ingredients together and spread half of the mixture to within ½ in. of edge of the pastry. Wet the edges and roll up using the greaseproof paper to help. Seal the edges. Place on a well oiled baking sheet. Brush with oil. Repeat the process with the rest of the pastry. Bake in the oven at 425°F, Mark 7, for 40 minutes. Turn down the oven after 30 minutes, if too brown. Cut into pieces and sprinkle with sifted icing (confectioner's) sugar.

note: apple strudel can also be made with rough puff pastry. See salmon rolls, page 113.

Kaese strudel

1 lb. (2⅔ cups) curd cheese
2 eggs
2 oz. (¼ cup) sugar
2 oz. (½ cup) sultanas (white raisins)
few drops of vanilla essence

Mix all the ingredients together.

Cherry and apricot strudel

Pitted cherries or apricots can be used instead of apples.

Kasha strudel (savoury)

Use Kasha mixture, see page 27.

Kasse strudel

4 oz. (8T) margarine
4 oz. (1 cup) plain (all purpose) flour
4 oz. (⅔ cup) curd cheese
icing (confectioners') sugar to sprinkle

filling
8 oz. (1⅓ cups) curd cheese
1 egg
2 oz. (¼ cup) sugar
2 oz. (¼ cup) sultanas (white raisins)

Rub the margarine into the flour. Add the cheese. Mix well to form dough. Chill.
Roll out the pastry very thinly into an oblong. Beat the cheese, egg, sugar and sultanas (white raisins) together into a smooth consistency. Spread the pastry with the filling to within ½ in. of the edge. Wet the edges. Roll up tightly. Bake on a greased sheet in the oven at 425°F, Mark 7, for 15 minutes, and then at 350°F, Mark 4, for another 15 minutes. Sprinkle with icing (confectioner's) sugar.

Linzer torte

4 oz. (8T) margarine
6 oz. (1½ cups) plain (all purpose) flour
3 oz. (¾ cup) ground almonds
3 oz. (⅜ cup) sugar
grated rind of ¼ lemon
pinch of cinnamon
2 drops of almond essence
1 egg
jam
icing (confectioners') sugar to sprinkle

Rub the margarine into the flour. Add the almonds, sugar, grated lemon rind and cinnamon. Mix the essence into the egg, and use sufficient to form a dough. Chill, if possible. Roll out and line an 8 in. flan dish. Spread with jam. Roll out the trimmings of pastry, and cut into strips. Make a lattice work over the jam, wetting the pastry edge to stick the strips. Bake in the oven at 350°F, Mark 4, for about 45 minutes. Dust with icing (confectioner's) sugar.

Linzer torte

Sponge cake

4 eggs
4 oz. (½ cup) sugar
4 oz. (1 cup) self raising flour

Grease a tin 11 × 7 in. and sprinkle with half a teaspoon of sugar and half a teaspoon of flour. Shake off the surplus. Warm a mixing bowl and add the sugar and eggs. Whip together until thick. Fold in the sieved flour carefully. Place in the tin and bake in the oven at 375°F, Mark 5, for 25 minutes.

Continental fruit cake

8 oz. (1 cup) margarine
6 oz. (¾ cup) castor (superfine) sugar
2 eggs, beaten
10 oz. (2½ cups) self raising flour

filling
2 oz. (4T) butter
2 oz. ($\frac{5}{16}$ cup) brown sugar
1 cooking apple, peeled and grated
2 oz. (½ cup) sultanas (white raisins)
2 oz. (½ cup) raisins
1 oz. (¼ cup) currants
1 teaspoon cinnamon

Cream together the margarine and sugar. Add the beaten eggs gradually. Fold in the sieved flour. Place the mixture in a well greased 7 in. tin, with the base lined with greaseproof paper. Bake in the oven at 350°F, Mark 4, for 1 hour.

filling: melting the butter and sugar together, add the rest of the filling ingredients and mix well.
When cool, split and spread with the filling.

Sweetmeats, preserves and pickles

Only in recent times have observant Jews been able to buy manufactured sweets and preserves which conformed to Jewish Dietary Laws, hence the strong habit of making them at home. The pickled items stem from the times when these things were a necessary requisite at almost every meal, but especially during the winter months, to make the duller foods more tasty.

Stuffed dates or prunes

filling
4 oz. (½ cup) cream cheese
1 oz. (¼ cup) chopped walnuts
3 oz. (¾ cup) ground almonds
3 oz. (¾ cup) sugar
yolk of egg
few drops of vanilla essence
few drops of almond essence
1 teaspoon lemon juice
few drops rose water, if possible
desiccated coconut or icing
(confectioner's) sugar to roll in

Mix ingredients together. Remove stones (pits), and stuff dates or soaked prunes with chosen ingredients. Roll in coconut or icing (confectioner's) sugar. Serve in paper cases.

Tayglech

Honey toffee

2 oz. (¼ cup) plain (all purpose) flour
pinch of salt
½ teaspoon ginger
1 egg
½ lb (⅔ cup) honey
chopped nuts or desiccated coconut

Mix together the flour, salt and ginger. Add the egg to mixture to form a dough. Roll into pencil thin ropes with floured hands. Cut into ¼ in. pieces to make tayglech.
Bring the honey to the boil in a small pan. Add the tayglech, a few at a time, then boil slowly until rich brown for about 15 minutes. Pour on to a wetted board. Flatten with a wet spoon. Sprinkle with the chopped nuts, and cut into squares when cool.

Almond cherries

4 oz. (1 cup) ground almonds
2 oz. (¼ cup) caster (superfine) sugar
2 oz. (⅜ cup) sifted icing (confectioner's) sugar
½ teaspoon lemon juice
yolk of egg
cherries
icing (confectioner's) sugar
finely grated chocolate or chocolate vermicelli
angelica

Mix together the almonds, sugar, juice and egg. Knead well. Take a small piece, the size of small walnut and roll into a ball and flatten. Put a cherry in the middle, and mould the almond paste around the cherry. Roll in icing (confectioner's) sugar and grated chocolate, or chocolate vermicelli. Decorate with a leaf of angelica.
Almond cherries can be dipped in melted chocolate instead of icing (confectioner's) sugar or grated chocolate.

Fruit balls

4 oz. (½ cup) stoned (pitted) dates
4 oz. (1 cup) stoned (pitted) raisins
4 oz. (⅔ cup) stoned (pitted) prunes
1 pear, peeled
4 oz. (1 cup) mixed nuts, chopped
pinch of cinnamon
½ tablespoon (¾T) orange juice
1 tablespoon (1¼T) lemon juice
extra chopped nuts, desiccated coconut or grated chocolate for rolling
angelica and glacé (candied) cherries for decoration
makes about 3 dozen

Mince (grind) all the ingredients together. Mix with the cinnamon and juices. Roll into small balls. Roll in the chopped nuts. Decorate with glacé (candied) cherries and angelica. Put into paper cases and leave to dry.

variations: other fruit and nuts can be used.
Apples can be used instead of pears.

Carrot ingberlach

1 lb. carrots **juice of 1 lemon** **1 lb. (2 cups) sugar** **2 oz. (¼ cup) almonds, chopped** **½ teaspoon ginger** **extra sugar**	Peel, wash and grate the carrots. Place on a sheet of foil with the lemon juice. Fold up tightly. Cook in the oven at 375°F, Mark 5, for 1 hour until tender. Turn into a saucepan, add the sugar, almonds and ginger. Cook slowly until thick, about 15–20 minutes. Test a little on a cold plate, when it sets hard it is cooked. Turn on to a sugared board. Sprinkle with sugar. Just before they are really hard, cut into squares or diamonds.

Pomerantzen
Crystallized (candied) orange rind

orange peel **sugar**	Remove all the pith from the peel. Cut the peel into strips ¼ in. wide, cover with cold water, and bring to the boil. Drain off the water. Repeat the process three times. Weigh the rind and take an equal amount of sugar. Place the rind and sugar in a pan with enough boiling water to cover. Boil gently until the rind is tender and clear. Cool, strain from the syrup and roll in granulated sugar. Lemon, grapefruit and citron peel should be allowed to soak in cold water for 24 hours to remove any bitterness, before proceeding as above. The cooled rind can be allowed to dry, then dipped into melted chocolate.

Lemon curd

2 eggs **4 oz. (½ cup) sugar** **2 oz. (4T) butter or margarine** **grated rind and juice of 2 lemons**	Beat the eggs in a basin. Add the sugar and butter in small pieces, grated lemon rind and juice of lemons. Stand the basin over a saucepan of water and heat slowly. Cook, stirring all the time until curd thickens. Sieve to remove the rind. Pour into jars, cover and label.

Chrane

4 oz. horseradish **2 oz. beetroot, cooked** **3 teaspoons acetic acid** **6 tablespoons (7½T) water** **pinch of salt** **pinch of sugar**	Scrub, peel and grate the horseradish, to make 1 cup approximately. Mix with the finely grated, cooked beetroot. Add the acetic acid, salt and sugar. Mix very well, or place all the ingredients in a liquidizer. Adjust the seasoning. Instead of cooked beetroot and acetic acid, the beetroot and liquor of beetroot rossel (see below) can be used.

Beetroot rossel

Beetroot **lukewarm boiled water**	Remove the tops, scrub and peel the beetroots. Slice, cover in stone crock or glass jar. Cover with lukewarm, boiled water to come 2 in. above the beetroots, cover with a lid. Remove the scum every week. Leave for 3–4 weeks. Use to add to borsht soup to improve flavour or to make chrane.

Pickled herrings

2 salt pickling herrings
1 onion
½ pint (1½ cups) boiling water, approx.
3 teaspoons acetic acid
½ tablespoon (¾T) sugar
1 bay leaf
1 teaspoon mixed pickling spices

Remove the heads, fins, and scales of the herrings. Wash thoroughly and leave to soak in cold water for 24 hours. If roll mops are required, also remove the bones. Peel and slice the onion. Pour enough boiling water over the onion to cover. Leave to cool. Rinse the herrings, and pack into a glass jar. For roll mops, roll boned herrings from head to tail with a slice of onion inside. Secure with cocktail stick. Add the cooled onions and the water, sugar, acetic acid and spices. Top up with more cool, boiled water to cover. Cover and leave in a cool larder (kitchen cabinet) for 2–3 days.

Haimishe Pickled cucumbers

3 lb. small Dutch ridge cucumbers, about 18
1 tablespoon (1¼T) pickling spice
2 bay leaves
3 cloves garlic or 3 sprays dill
brine, made by dissolving 4 oz. (½ cup) salt in 2 pints (5 cups) water

Wash and trim the cucumbers. Pack in a large glass jar or a stone crock. Sprinkle with the pickling spice, bay leaves, and cut up garlic or dill. Cover completely with the brine (use more than 2 pints (5 cups) if required, according to shape of jar). See that cucumbers are completely immersed by putting a saucer or dish on top. Cover with greaseproof paper. Leave for about a week.

Red cabbage

1 red cabbage, about 2 lb.
salt
1 tablespoon (1¼T) pickling spice
2 pints (5 cups) vinegar

Remove the outer leaves of the cabbage, cut into four and remove thick stalks. Wash very carefully, drain and shred finely. Place the shredded cabbage in a thin layer on a flat dish and sprinkle with salt. Leave for 24 hours.
Boil the vinegar and spices together, and allow to cool. Place the cabbage in a colander, rinse quickly to remove excess salt, shake dry. Pack into jars and cover completely with the cold, strained, spiced vinegar. Cover tightly with greaseproof paper. Leave for about 1 week.

Raisin wine

1 lb. (4 cups) raisins
4 pints (10 cups) water
½ lb. (1 cup) sugar

Liquidize the raisins and ¼ pint (½ cup + 2T) water to just macerate raisins. Add the sugar and the rest of the water. Heat until nearly boiling. Stir well, and place in a large glass jar. Leave for a week, stirring very well each day. Strain through muslin, pressing the raisins well to extract all the juice, then bottle and label.
Can be used in 2 weeks.

Med Mead

2 well heaped tablespoons (2½T generous) hops
½ lb. (⅔ cup) honey
2 pints (5 cups) water
slice of lemon

Place the hops in a muslin bag. Put all the ingredients in a large saucepan, and bring to the boil. Simmer for 30 minutes. Remove the scum from time to time.
Allow to cool and strain through muslin into a large glass jar, stone crock or wooden cask. Do not fill the container more than three quarters full to allow for fermentation. Cover with muslin and leave until the fermentation stops in about 3 weeks. Pour into bottles and cork, or leave in the jar, also corked. Label and store in a cool, dark place.

Reception bites and Kiddush items

Occasions for a celebration come thick and fast in Jewish homes. There is the Kiddush, a benediction over wine, which takes place after the Sabbath or Festival morning service. The food served at a Kiddush may be simply wine, sweet cake and biscuits. More elaborately, it might be small savoury bite-sized delicacies.

Other traditional occasions for celebration include:

Brit: the circumcision of a baby boy on the eighth day after he is born.

Shalem Zachor: a festive occasion for the family which takes place on the first Friday evening after the birth of a boy to welcome him into the family. Sweet things and nahit (chick peas) are traditionally served.

Pidyon Ha Ben: When a baby boy is the first-born, the Pidyon Ha Ben takes place when he is a month old. This means 'redemption of the first-born male'.

Bar Mitzvah: The coming of age of a boy at thirteen years, a ceremony in the Synagogue at which Jewish boys are called up to the reading of the Law. This is considered a very important event in a young man's life and a special birthday party usually takes place.

Engagement or T'Nayim. When a young Jewish couple become engaged, traditionally a contract or 'declaration of intent' is written and a toast is drunk to the future.

Wedding. A Jewish wedding combines solemnity and rejoicing. The bride and groom are married by a Rabbi under a Chuppah (marriage canopy). After the ceremony and the blessing the bridegroom crushes a glass with his foot. This startling act serves two purposes. One, to remind people of the solemnity of the occasion and two, to remind all present of the destruction of the Temple in Jerusalem and that in the midst of joy they should recall the sadness of the Jews at that time.

Chanukat Habayit is the celebration for the family in their new home—a 'housewarming' or a 'dedication of the home'. A Messuzah is fixed to the top right-hand side of the front door and each door inside the house. This contains small scrolls in Hebrew with two extracts from Deuteronomy. Prayers are said and bread and salt are brought into the house before the festivities commence.

Pirogen or Piroshki I

8 oz. (2 cups) self raising flour
pinch of salt and pepper
5 oz. (⅝ cup) margarine
1–2 eggs, saving some for
the glaze

makes 12 using a 3½ in. cutter.

Mix together the flour, salt and pepper. Rub in the margarine. Make into a stiff dough with the eggs.
Knead lightly and roll out thinly. Cut into rounds. Put teaspoonful of filling on the pastry. Wet the edges and fold into a half-moon shape, or bring the edges together to make a triangle shape. Brush with the beaten egg. Bake in the oven at 425°F, Mark 7, for 20–30 minutes. Pirogen can be fried in hot oil instead of baking.

Piroshki or pirogen II

1 oz. (2T) margarine
½ lb. (1 cup) potatoes, cooked
and mashed
4 oz. (1 cup) self raising flour
pinch of salt and pepper
1 egg

Makes 12 using a 3½ in. cutter.

Mix the margarine into the potatoes. Add the flour, salt and pepper, and make into a stiff dough with the egg.
Knead and roll out and cut into rounds. Place a teaspoon of filling in the middle of the pastry round. Wet the edges, fold in half to form into half circles. Seal well. Crimp the edges, and drop into boiling, salted water for 10–15 minutes; or bake on a greased tin for 15–20 minutes in the oven at 425°F, Mark 7.

Knishes

Use Pirogen pastry, see above

Roll out the pastry thinly to form an oblong. Spread the filling over the pastry to within ½ in. of the edge. Wet the edges, and roll up tightly. Cut into 1 in. thick pieces. Place cut side down on a well greased baking tin. Bake in the oven at 375°F, Mark 5, for ½ hour. Cheese Knishes are sometimes called Beiglach.

Varenikes

Kreplach dough, see page 125

Roll out the kreplach dough very thinly. Cut into circles. Place small portions of filling on each circle. Wet the edges, fold over, and seal very well, crimping the edges.
Boil in salted water for ½ hour. Drain, and place in a well greased dish. Dot with fat and bake in the oven to brown.

Milk fillings for kreplach, varenikes, knishes, pirogen or piroshki

8 oz. (1⅓ cup) curd
(cottage) cheese
1 oz. (¼ cup) plain (all
(purpose) flour
1 egg
pinch of salt and pepper

Mix all the ingredients together.

8 oz. (1⅓ cup) curd
(cottage) cheese
1 egg
2 tablespoons (2½T) sugar, or
to taste

Mix all the ingredients together.

Meat fillings for kreplach, varenikes, knishes and pirogen or piroshki

meat
8 oz. (2 cups) cooked, minced, (ground) meat or liver
1 egg
1 grated raw, or fried onion
salt
pepper
garlic to taste

Mix all ingredients together.

potato
8 oz. (1 cup) cooked and mashed potato
1 egg
2 tablespoons (2½T) fried onions and minced grieven (crackling)
salt
pepper

Mix all ingredients together.

kasha
1 cup cooked kasha
2 tablespoons (2½T) fried onions
salt
pepper

Mix all the ingredients together.

lung and liver

See Lung and Liver Pie, page 50.

Mincedmeat rolls

4 oz. pastry, see mushroom tarts, below i.e. made from 4 oz. flour
8 oz. minced (ground) beef
¼ teaspoon garlic salt
pinch of pepper
2 tablespoons (2½T) matzo meal
1 egg

Roll out the pastry into an oblong 12 × 4 in. Mix all the other ingredients together, reserving a little egg for glazing. Place filling along the length of the pastry, leaving ½ in. on one side and 1½ in. on the other. Damp the edges, and fold over the pastry, sealing well. Brush with egg and cut into even lengths. Bake in the oven at 425°F, Mark 7, for 20–30 minutes.

Mushroom tartlets

pastry
8 oz. (2 cups) plain (all purpose) flour
pinch of salt
5 oz. (⅝ cup) margarine
2 tablespoons (2½T) cold water, approximately
if preferred, the pastry can be bound with a beaten egg instead of water

filling
4 oz. (1 cup) button mushrooms
2 oz. (¼ cup) margarine
½ teaspoon finely grated onion
squeeze of lemon
1 oz. (¼ cup) flour
½ pint less 2 tablespoons (1¼ cups less 2½T) milk
salt and pepper to taste
makes approximately 18 tartlets.

Mix together the flour and salt. Rub in the margarine and mix to a very stiff dough with as little water, or egg, as possible. Roll out thinly, and cut into rounds and line tartlet tins. Prick with a fork. Bake in the oven at 425°F, Mark 7, for 7–15 minutes.
Wash, dry and slice the mushrooms and cook them gently in a saucepan with ½ oz. (1T) margarine, onions and lemon juice. Put the mixture on to a plate. Melt the rest of the margarine in the saucepan, add the flour and cook for half a minute, but do not brown. Remove the saucepan from the heat and add the milk gradually. Bring to the boil and cook for 1 minute. Add the mushrooms and any liquor. Season to taste. Just before serving, place a teaspoonful of the sauce in the baked tartlet cases, and reheat thoroughly in a slow oven.

Salmon rolls

pastry
4 oz. (1 cup) plain (all purpose) flour
3 oz. (⅜ cup) hard margarine, from the refrigerator
pinch of salt
1 teaspoon lemon juice or vinegar
cold water to mix

filling
1 medium (7½ oz.) can salmon
shake of pepper
1 small onion, grated
1 egg
2 tablespoons (2½ T) matzo meal

For method see Vegetable Strudel, page 59.

Mix the contents of the can of salmon with the pepper, onion and egg, and sufficient matzo meal to make into a soft mixture, reserving some of the egg to glaze the pastry.

Roll out the pastry into a long strip about 12 × 4 in. Damp the edges. Place the filling along the length of the pastry, leaving ½ in. at the edge, and 1½ in. on the other edge. Fold over the pastry and seal edges. Trim, and knock up the edge. Brush with the egg. Snip top to decorate and cut into even lengths. Bake in the oven at 450°F, Mark 8, for 15–20 minutes on a damp tray.

Curd (cottage) cheese biscuits and
Onion biscuits (left) Salmon rolls (right)

Curd (cottage) cheese savoury biscuits

4 oz. (8T) margarine
4 oz. (1 cup) plain (all purpose) flour
4 oz. (⅔ cup) curd (cottage) cheese
pinch of salt
egg for glaze
paprika
makes about 30 2 in. biscuits.

Rub the margarine into the flour. Add the cheese and salt. Knead lightly and chill. Roll out the pastry quite thickly and cut into small rounds. Brush with the beaten egg. Bake in the oven at 425°F, Mark 7, for 10–15 minutes.
Serve hot, sprinkled with paprika.

Onion biscuits

5 oz. (⅝ cup) margarine
8 oz. (2 cups) plain (all purpose) flour
1 finely grated onion
⅛ teaspoon salt
pinch of pepper
1 egg
extra egg for glaze
poppy seed, optional
makes about 2 dozen 2 in. biscuits.

Rub the margarine into the flour. Add the onion and seasoning. Mix to a stiff dough with sufficient beaten egg. Knead lightly. Roll out and cut into squares. Brush with the beaten egg. Sprinkle with poppy seed, if liked. Bake in the oven at 400°F, Mark 6, for 15–20 minutes.

Red cabbage (opposite above left)

Pickled cucumbers (opposite above right)

left: Fruit balls; right: Pomerantzen; bottom: Stuffed dates and prunes (opposite)

front: Avocado dip; back: Houmous (above)

Boobelach (left)

Bridge rolls

½ oz. fresh yeast (½ cake compressed yeast), or ¼ oz. (2 teaspoons) dried yeast
1 teaspoon sugar
2 tablespoons (2½T) warm water
8 oz. (2 cups) plain (all purpose) flour
½ teaspoon salt
1 oz. (2T) margarine
1 egg
warm water
egg and 1 teaspoon sugar for glaze
makes about 18.

Mix together the yeast, teaspoon sugar, and 2 tablespoons (2½T) water. Leave in a warm place until bubbly. Mix together the flour and salt, and rub in margarine. Mix the egg with the yeast water. Pour this mixture into the centre of the flour, using more warm water, if necessary, to make into a soft dough. Beat well. Knead on a board until smooth.
Cut the dough into three, and with the hands roll into ropes about ¾ in. thick × 12 in. long. Cut into pieces about 2 in. long. Pinch the ends to shape into ovals. Place on greased tins, and brush with water. Place the tins in a greased polythene bag. Leave to rise in a warm place until doubled in size. Brush with the beaten egg mixture with 1 teaspoon of sugar. Bake in the oven at 425°F, Mark 7, for 15 minutes. The egg wash can be omitted if the rolls are to be used open.

Avocado dip

1 avocado pear
1 tablespoon (1¼T) lemon juice
salt and pepper to taste
1 tablespoon (1¼T) mayonnaise
1 teaspoon chopped onion or chopped leek

Cut the avocado pear in half, and remove the stone. Scoop out the flesh and mash with the rest of the ingredients. Serve on bridge rolls, biscuits or as a dip.

Houmous

4 oz. (½ cup) chick peas
¼ teaspoon garlic salt
¼ teaspoon salt
shake of pepper
juice of 1 lemon
¼ teaspoon paprika
2 tablespoons olive oil, approximately
black olives and parsley for garnish

Soak the peas overnight. Cook until tender, about 1 hour, in salted water. Liquidize the peas with the seasonings, lemon juice and oil. Add more oil to make into a soft creamy consistency. Adjust the seasoning.
Serve in a small dish garnished with olives and parsley.

Cream cheese spreads

4 oz. (½ cup) cream cheese
mixed with about 1 teaspoon (or
to taste) of finely chopped leek,
chives, or spring onion (scallion).

4 oz. (½ cup) cream cheese
mixed with paprika to colour,
and a pinch of garlic salt.

4 oz. (½ cup) cream cheese
mixed with 1 tablespoon (1¼T)
chopped walnuts

4 oz. (½ cup) cream cheese
1 tablespoon (1¼T) finely
chopped green pepper

To make into dips, add 1 tablespoon (1¼T) of top-of-the-milk, or 1 tablespoon (1¼T) sour cream.

Spring cheese dip

½ lb. (1⅓ cup) curd cheese
top-of-the-milk, or smetana
1 tablespoon (1¼T) finely
sliced radishes
1 tablespoon (1¼T) chopped
spring onions (scallions),
or chives
salt
pepper

Add sufficient top-of-the-milk or smetana to the curd cheese to make a soft mixture. Beat until smooth. Add the radishes, spring onions (scallions), or chives. Mix well, and season with salt and pepper to taste.
Serve on lettuce leaves for a salad, decorate with tomatoes, or use for a cheese dip with crisps, celery or black bread.

Cream cheese mayonnaise

½ lb. (1 cup) cream cheese
4 tablespoons (5T) mayonnaise
1 tablespoon (1¼T) chopped
chives and watercress
pepper and salt

Cream all the ingredients together, and season to taste.

alternatives: finely chopped chicory, celery, pimento, cucumber, leeks. Serve as a dip, or as a salad with lettuce and eggs.

Liptauer cheese dip

½ lb. (1⅓ cup) curd cheese, or a
mixture of ½ curd and ½ cream
cheese
top-of-the-milk (light cream)
1 small pickled
cucumber, chopped
5 black or green olives, chopped
2 anchovy fillets, chopped
½ teaspoon caraway seeds
paprika

Add sufficient top-of-the-milk (light cream) to the curd cheese to moisten, and mix well. Add the chopped cucumber, olives, anchovies, caraway seeds, and paprika to colour. Beat all ingredients together. Serve on water biscuits or toast, or as a dip with crisps, brown or black bread.

Nahit (chick peas) or bobs (brown beans)

Wash ½ lb. (1 cup) chick peas or brown beans. Put in a bowl, and cover with boiling water, leaving to soak for 12 hours. Rinse and put them into a pan with cold water to cover. Bring to the boil and simmer for 1–2 hours, or longer, until they are tender. Drain, and dust with salt.
Serve hot or cold.

The Sabbath

Shabbat—the Jewish Sabbath—commences at dusk on Friday
evening and closes with the appearance of the first three stars on
Saturday evening. A most important Jewish family festival, taking
place every week throughout the year. Shabbat includes three
obligatory meals—Friday night dinner, Saturday lunch and Shalosh
Se'uda, or third meal (usually high tea or supper). The eve of
Sabbath (Friday night) meal and table setting symbolizes in a way
the whole of Judaism and Jewish observance: the candlesticks, and
Kiddush wine goblet, the two Challahs (plaited loaves) covered with
an embroidered Challah cloth, the salt and wine for the Kiddush
ceremony with which the Sabbath begins.

No cooking is permitted for observant Jews on the Sabbath, so any
food required hot for Saturday lunch has to be prepared on Friday
and cooking commenced before the Sabbath comes in. This is the
origin of the slow-cooked meat and vegetable casserole called
Cholent.

The Shalosh Se'uda, or obligatory third meal, takes place in the early
evening of the Sabbath and precedes the evening prayer. A cold meal,
this high tea often includes fried fish, pickled herring and salads.

Friday night menus:

Gehakte Leber	**Eggs and Onions**
Goldene Yoich and Mandelen	**Borsht and Sour Cream**
Roast Stuffed Chicken	**Gefillte Fish**
Potato Pompishkes	**Potato Salad**
Honeyed Carrots	**Kol Bo Salad**
Apricot Whip	**Baklava**

Sabbath lunch menu	**Sabbath evening menu**
Petcha	**Grapefruit and Sour Cream**
Cholent	**Cold Fried Fish and Salad**
Aufschnitt (cold cuts) of Salt Beef	**Cous Cous**
Tongue and Chicken	**Almond Biscuits**
Salads	**Tea or Coffee**
Apple Strudel	

Eve of Sabbath table setting

Challah

½ oz. fresh yeast (½ cake compressed yeast) or ¼ oz. (2 teaspoons) dried yeast
1 teaspoon sugar
warm water
1 lb. (4 cups) strong plain (all purpose) flour
1 teaspoon salt
2 tablespoons (2½T) oil
1 egg
poppy seeds
beaten egg to glaze

Mix together the yeast, sugar and 2 tablespoons (2½T) warm water and leave until bubbly, 5–10 minutes. Mix together the flour and salt. Make a well in centre of the flour and add one egg, yeast mixture and enough warm water gradually to make into a stiff dough. Beat very well.

Turn on to a board, and knead for 5 minutes. Divide into eight. Knead each piece and roll into a long strip. Make into two loaves by plaiting. Place on a greased and floured tin. Brush with water. Slip into a greased polythene bag and leave in a warm place until doubled in size.

Brush with the beaten egg and sprinkle with poppy seeds. Bake in the oven at 400°F, Mark 6, for 10 minutes, then reduce heat to 350°F, Mark 4, for 45 minutes. The unbaked Challah can be left in a refrigerator overnight in the polythene bag and then put in a warm place until doubled in size the next day, before baking.

taking challah: if three of more pounds of flour are made into dough for bread 'Challah' has to be taken. A small portion of the dough not less than the size of an olive) is removed and the following blessing is recited:

'Blessed art thou Lord our God,
King of the Universe who sanctified
us with His commandments and ordered
us to set apart the Bread.'

Challah

The piece of dough is then burnt.

Cholent

4 oz. (½ cup) haricot beans,
soaked for a few hours, or
barley, or a mixture of both
1 onion, sliced
1 carrot, sliced
1 lb. top rib or other fatty meat
4 potatoes, sliced
boiling water, to cover
salt, 1 teaspoon to each pint
(2½ cups) of water, or to taste
pepper to taste
stuffed neck (optional), see
page 52)
or dumpling (optional), see
Kneidlach recipe page 29)
serves 4–6

Put the beans or barley in the bottom of a deep casserole with the
onion and carrot and lay the meat on top. Arrange the sliced
potatoes (and stuffed neck or dumpling, if used) around the meat.
Pour the boiling water over to cover and add the salt and pepper.
Cover with a tightly fitting lid.

Cook for 2 hours in the oven at 400°F, Mark 5, before the Sabbath
commences, and then turn down to lowest marking to continue
cooking until Sabbath lunch; or the Cholent can be put on the top of
the stove before the Sabbath commences, the flame being completely
covered by a sheet of tin or asbestos.

Havdallah candle, wine cup and
spice box (Sabbath)

Typical family meals

A family meal in an orthodox Jewish home would be either completely 'meat' or completely 'milk'. The following three typical menus, chosen from recipes in this book, are two 'meat' meals and one 'milk' meal.

Hubagrits Soup
Sauerbraten, Baked Potatoes
Einbren of Peas and Carrots
Apple Shalet

Aubergine Pâté
Schwemelach and Barley Soup
Stuffed Breast of Lamb
Baked Rice and Potatoes
Fresh Fruit

Smetana Soup
Spiced Baked Fish
Green salad
Lochshen Pudding

Sabbath meal. Top, left to right: Potato salad. Apple flan. Apricot whip. Centre, left to right: Mandlen. Tomato salad. Carrots. Pineapple, Celery and Walnut salad. Chopped liver. Gefillte fish. Borsht. Bottom, left to right: Roast chicken. Savoury rice.

The Jewish New Year

This festival takes place in the autumn. Jews pray for happiness in the year to come. Foods associated with Rosh Hashanah are honey and honey cake (Lekach), apples and all sorts of apple dishes, and carrots made into sweet dishes. Honey cake and sweet wine are served to symbolize 'sweetness' in the New Year.

Honey cake lekach

1 lb. (1¼ cup) honey
⅜ pint (1 cup) oil
2 teaspoons instant coffee dissolved in ¼ pint (½ cup+2T) boiling water
½ lb. (1¼ cups) dark brown sugar
4 eggs
1 lb. (4 cups) self raising flour
1 heaped teaspoon each, cinnamon, and mixed spice
1 level teaspoon each, ginger and bicarbonate of soda (baking soda)

Beat together the honey, oil, coffee and sugar. Beat in the eggs. Beat in the rest of the ingredients sifted together. Bake in a greased, shallow tin 12 × 10 × 3 in. in the oven at 325°F, Mark 3, for 1–1¼ hours.

top: Honey and apples, the foods of sweetness and happiness, with the shofar or ram's horn (Rosh Hashanah)

right: Rosh Hashanah (Honey cake lekach)

Day of Atonement

Yom Kippur comes ten days after the New Year. It is a fast day, and the most holy day in the Jewish calendar. The eve of Yom Kippur is the occasion for a special meal in which no highly spiced items are served, but bland foods which will fit the family for the fast of twenty-five hours ahead of them. This day is spent in the synagogue when Jews pray for forgiveness. Typical foods served on the eve of Yom Kippur are Chicken Soup (Goldene Yoich), poultry, apple pies and Apple Strudel and Kreplach.

After the fast is over most families have their own favourite menus, which might contain some of the following: pickled and chopped herrings, olives, pickled cucumbers, fried fish and gefillte fish and all types of salads. Some families, however, prefer a full chicken dinner.

Kreplach

dough
1 egg
pinch of salt
pinch of pepper
3 oz. (¾ cup) flour, approximately

filling
8 oz. (1 cup) cooked meat or liver
1 small onion, grated, raw or fried
1 egg
pinch of salt
pinch of pepper
makes 18 kreplach.

Beat together the egg and seasonings. Gradually beat in enough flour to form a stiff dough. Knead well, and roll out very thinly. Leave to dry for about 1 hour. Cut into 3 in. squares.

Mix together the filling ingredients. Place a portion of the filling in the centre of each square. Wet the edges and fold over to form a triangle. Seal well and then press the two longer points together. Leave to dry for about 30 minutes. Drop into gently boiling, salted water, or soup and simmer for 15 minutes. Serve in chicken soup. These can be served as a separate course as well, with a mushroom or tomato sauce.

osite: Pesach/Passover (top: Pesach puffs, bottom: Plava)   above: Strudel for Succoth   below: Tu B'Shevat (fruit salad)

Feast of Tabernacles

This festival of late autumn commemorates the Biblical time when the Jews left Egypt to wander in the desert before reaching the Promised Land. They then lived in makeshift huts or 'Succoth' and observant Jews today build such a structure out of wood and branches with the roof intertwined with leaves, and harvest fruits—yet open to the skies.

The family eat their meals in the 'Succah' which has been decorated with vegetables and autumn fruits by all the family.

During the Succoth festival four symbolic objects are used—the esrog (a type of citrus), the luluv (palm branch), the hadassim (myrtle) and arovot (willow) twigs. These form part of the Succoth synagogue service when Jews give thanks for the fruits of the earth.

Strudel for Succoth

2 oz. (½ cup) self raising flour
2 oz. (½ cup) plain (all purpose) flour
pinch of salt
2 tablespoons (2½T) oil
1 teaspoon lemon juice
4 tablespoons (5T) boiling water
extra oil
sugar to sprinkle

filling
4 tablespoons (5T) biscuit crumbs
6 level tablespoons (7½T) jam
3 oz. (¾ cup) currants and sultanas, mixed
2 oz. (½ cup) nuts, chopped
1 level tablespoon (1¼T) soft brown sugar
1 teaspoon cinnamon
grated rind and juice of 1 lemon

Place the flour and salt in a bowl. Add the oil, lemon juice and water and form a soft dough. Knead well, and leave for 30 minutes covered by a warm bowl. Divide into two. On large sheet of floured, greaseproof paper roll until very thin. Place your hands under the pastry and pull even thinner.

Mix all the filling ingredients together. Brush the pastry with oil and spread with half of the filling. Wet the edges and roll up using the paper to help. Brush with oil, and sprinkle with the sugar. Place on a well oiled tin. Repeat with the remaining pastry. Bake in the oven at 325°F, Mark 3, for 1–1¼ hours until brown. Baste with the oil from the baking tin from time to time.

Traditionally decorated Succah (Succoth)

Rejoicing of the Law

This festival, which celebrates the completion of the reading of the law and its new beginning, has special attractions for children. In the synagogue children join in a procession waving Simchat Torah flags topped with apples. When the service is over the children receive gifts of sweets, cakes and fruit. Special dishes associated with this festival are Holishkes and stuffed peppers and, in some countries, grape vine leaves stuffed with minced (ground) meat.

Ollipses or holishkes Stuffed cabbage

12 large cabbage leaves
1 lb. (2 cups) minced (ground) meat
2 tablespoons (2½T) matzo meal
2 large onions, minced (ground)
1 oz. (2T) chicken fat or margarine
1 carrot, minced (ground)
1 tablespoons (1¼T) golden syrup
stock to cover
grated rind and juice of 1 lemon
1 teaspoon vinegar
extra sugar and lemon to taste
serves 4 as a main course.

Blanch the washed cabbage leaves by pouring boiling water over them. Remove the hard stalks. Mix together the meat, matzo meal and half the minced (ground) onions. Place a portion of the meat mixture on to each leaf and roll up like a parcel. Melt the fat in a pan and fry the remainder of the minced (ground) onion and carrot. Add the syrup and cook for 1 minute to brown a little. Add the cabbage rolls and enough stock to cover them. Add the salt, lemon juice and grated rind, and vinegar. Cook very slowly for 3 hours. Adjust the seasoning to taste.

Serve as a main course with plain boiled rice, or as a forspeis (hors d'oeuvre).

note: cooking in the oven—cook for about 3 hours at 325°F, Mark 3. Choose a casserole with a tightly fitting lid. Or cook overnight at 225°F, Mark ¼.

top: Children's sweets and candies (Simchat Torah)

right: Simchat Torah (Holishkes)

Festival of Lights

This holiday takes place in midwinter and marks the rededication by the Jews of the holy temple in Jerusalem after its desecration by the Greeks. During this festival, which lasts eight days, one candle is lit in a candelabra— the Menorah—on the first night, and on each succeeding night an additional candle is lit until eight are lit on the last night. Children usually receive gifts of money (Chanukah Gelt). Popular Chanukah foods are grated potato latkes (pancakes) and doughnuts.

Menorah and spinning tops (Chanukah)

Doughnuts

½ oz. fresh yeast (½ cake compressed yeast), or ¼ oz. (2 teaspoons) dried yeast
2 tablespoons (2½T) warm water
1 oz. (⅛ cup) sugar
8 oz. (2 cups) strong plain (all purpose) flour
½ teaspoon salt
1 oz. (2T) butter or margarine
1 egg, beaten
about ⅛ pint (¼ cup+1T) warm milk or water
oil for frying
jam
castor (superfine) sugar

Mix together the yeast, warm water and 1 teaspoonful of the sugar, and leave to stand until bubbly. Sift the flour and salt into a bowl. Rub in the fat. Make a well in the flour mixture and add the yeast mixture with the beaten egg, and enough warm milk or water to make a soft dough. Beat well and then knead for 5 minutes on a floured board.

Divide into twelve pieces, knead each well and place apart on a greased and floured tin. Brush with water and place the tin in a greased polythene bag and leave until they have doubled in size. This will take about 1 hour in a warm place.

Fry in oil that is not too hot 350°F–360°F, turning over to brown both sides, about 3 minutes. Drain on absorbent paper. With the handle of a spoon make a hole in the side of the doughnut and insert the jam. Roll in castor (superfine) sugar.

To serve as a sweet, split in half, fill with whipped cream and decorate with nuts and serve with orange sauce, see page 70.

New Year for Trees

A one-day festival coinciding with the blossoming of trees in Israel, Tu B'Shevat occurs towards the end of winter. In Israel today saplings are planted to mark the occasion and all sorts of fruits are eaten.

Young sapling planted for the festival (Tu B'Shevat)

Tu b'shevat fruit salad

**a selection of fruits such as:
fresh fruits—oranges, apricots,
grapes, apples, pears,
bananas, plums
dried fruits—dates, raisins,
prunes, nuts
To make up the number, see if
you can obtain any luxury fresh
Israeli fruits, such as
strawberries, or canned fruits
In addition, orange and lemon
juice, sherry, brown sugar,
flaked chocolate, optional**

Prepare each fruit for eating. Slice and sprinkle the apples, pears, bananas with lemon juice to prevent browning. Chop the dried fruits and blanched nuts and soak in the sherry.

Mix all the fruits together leaving a few choice pears for decoration. Add a little orange juice and some brown sugar, if liked. The mixture should not be too sweet but should be quite moist. Arrange in glass bowl, cover with foil, refrigerate for a few hours allowing the flavours to blend. Sprinkle with the flaked chocolate and decorate.

Feast of Lots

Sometimes called the Feast of Esther. Purim joyously celebrates the downfall of the tyrant, Haman, through the efforts of Mordecai and his niece, Queen Esther. A very happy festival, Purim is the occasion of present-giving, plays, and dressing-up for children, games and great merry-making. The waving of noisy Purim gregars (rattles) is traditional and at the festival meal the foods would include the Purim Kalisch (decorated sweet plaited loaf) taking place of honour at the festive meal, and Hamantaschen, triangular pastries filled with poppy seeds, and bobs (brown beans).

Masks, gregars and a megillah containing Purim prayers (Purim)

Hamantaschen (right)

Hamantaschen

5 oz. (⅝ cup) margarine
5 oz. (⅝ cup) sugar
1 egg
4 oz. (1 cup) self raising flour
4 oz. (1 cup) plain (all purpose) flour
melted honey to glaze
coloured strands (confectioners' decorations) to sprinkle

Cream together the margarine and sugar until soft. Add the yolk of egg and the flour slowly to make a very stiff dough, using some egg white if dry. Knead lightly. Roll out thinly, and cut into 3 in. rounds. Place the filling in the centre of each round. Brush the edges with water, and bring the edges to the centre to form triangles. Bake in the oven at 425°F, Mark 7, for 20 minutes.

Brush with melted honey and sprinkle with coloured strands (confectioners' decorations).

filling
4 oz. (⅓ cup) poppy seeds, ground
grated lemon rind
¼ pint (½ cup+2T) water
2 oz. (¼ cup) sugar
1 oz. (2T) margarine
1 oz. (¼ cup) sultanas
a little wine, if liked
makes about 2 dozen

Simmer the poppy seeds in water with the other ingredients until thick. Use when cool.

Cheese bun dough can also be used.

The hamantaschen can be spread with glacé icing and then sprinkled with coloured strands.

Alternative filling

4 oz. (1 cup) sultanas
4 oz. (1 cup) raisins
2 oz. (½ cup) currants
2 oz. (¼ cup) sugar
1 teaspoon cinnamon
1 cooking apple, peeled and cored
juice and rind of 1 lemon

Mince (grind) all the ingredients together and mix well.

Prune filling

8 oz. (1⅓ cups) prunes
rind of 1 lemon and 1 orange
2 oz. (5/16 cup) brown sugar, or to taste

Soak the prunes overnight with the rinds and sugar and sufficient water to cover. Cook gently until the liquid has evaporated. Remove the rinds and stones, and chop finely or mince (grind).

note: drained, canned prunes may be used, mixed with finely grated lemon or orange rind.

Passover

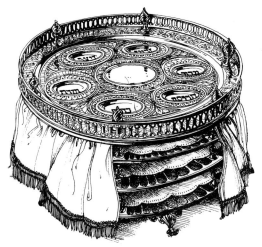

Seder plate (Passover)

This eight-day Spring festival celebrates the freeing of the Jewish people from slavery in Egypt. During the first two evenings of the festival—the Seder nights—Jews read from the Haggadah the Passover story. This tells of when they left Egypt in haste unable to bake their bread properly and instead baked Matzot or unleavened bread. During the period of Passover, only Matzot or unleavened bread is eaten and no foods containing leaven are allowed. In fact, before the Passover, the whole house is cleaned and on the night before Passover starts, a symbolic search throughout the house for Chametz (leaven) takes place. Foods eaten at Passover must have been manufactured under the supervision of a recognized Rabbinate. Special sets of 'milk' and 'meat' cooking utensils, crockery, cutlery and koshering equipment are reserved for use at Pesach only.

Typical of Pesach foods are those using matzo meal, potato flour and lots of eggs.

Pesach lochshen

2 eggs
salt and pepper
oil for frying

Beat the eggs, and add the seasoning.
Place a little oil in a frying pan (skillet). When the oil is hot pour in a little egg to cover base of the pan, when cooked, turn over and cook the other side. Turn on to a flat plate. Repeat the process until the mixture is finished.
Roll up each pancake and cut into strips (lochshen). Drop into boiling soup and cook for 2 minutes and serve.

Pesach puffs

¼ pint (½ cup+2T) water
1½ oz. (3T) margarine
¼ teaspoon salt
4 oz. (1 cup) fine matzo meal
3 eggs

vanilla cream
2 oz. (4T) margarine
4 oz. (¾ cup) icing
(confectioners') sugar
1 envelope vanilla sugar, if
available for Passover
1 tablespoon (1¼T)
top-of-the-milk or wine

chocolate icing
2 oz. (2 squares) plain chocolate
1 oz. (2T) margarine
1 tablespoon (1¼T) brandy
or wine
2 oz. (⅜ cup) icing
(confectioners') sugar
1 tablespoon (1¼T) cocoa

Bring the water, margarine and salt to the boil. Pour over the matzo meal, stirring well. Cool slightly. Add the eggs one at a time to the matzo meal, and beat very well.
Place dessertspoonsful (tablespoonsful) of the mixture on a greased tin and bake for 40 minutes in the oven at 375°F, Mark 5. When cooked slit open and put back in the turned off oven to dry off. When cool fill them with vanilla cream. Spread with chocolate icing or dredge with icing (confectioner's) sugar. Serve in paper cases.

vanilla cream: cream together the margarine and sugars until very soft. Beat in the milk or wine.

chocolate icing: melt the chocolate and margarine over hot water. Add the brandy and beat in the icing (confectioner's) sugar and cocoa.

Spinach and matzo bake

2 oz. (4T) melted butter
or margarine
3 eggs
pinch of pepper
¼ teaspoon salt
3 matzot dipped in cold water
2 lb. spinach, washed well and
cooked in only the water
clinging to the leaves, drained,
chopped, well seasoned, and
mixed with a grated fried onion
4 oz. (1 cup) grated cheese

serves 4.

Put half the butter in a square dish and spread it round the sides. Beat together the eggs, pepper and salt. Dip a matzo in the beaten egg, and place in the dish which should be same size as matzo; if not cut an additional matzo to fill dish. Spread with half the spinach and a third of the grated cheese.
Dip a second matzo in the egg and place over the spinach and cheese. Add the rest of the spinach and sprinkle with a third of the cheese. Dip the last matzo in the egg, and place over spinach and cheese, pour over the rest of the butter and beaten egg, and sprinkle with the rest of the cheese. Bake in the oven at 375°F, Mark 5, for 30 minutes. The spinach and matzo bake can be cut into 1 in. squares and served as a cocktail savoury.
Fried onions and sliced skinned tomatoes can be used instead of spinach.

Boobelach

3 eggs
⅜ pint (1 cup) water,
approximately
½ teaspoon salt
4 oz. (1 cup) fine matzo meal
oil for frying
sugar and cinnamon to serve

Beat together the eggs, water and salt. Gradually mix in the meal to make a thick batter, using more water if necessary. Fry dessert-spoonsful (tablespoonsful) of the mixture in hot oil on both sides until brown. Drain on absorbent paper.
Serve with sugar and cinnamon.

note: pepper can be added and Boobelach can be served as an accompaniment to soup or meat.

Zwiebel matzot   Onion matzot

Rub each matzot on both sides with the cut side of an onion. Spread with chicken fat and a little salt. Place in hot oven for a few minutes to heat through, or heat under grill.
Serve as a soup accompaniment.

Matzo kleis

2 matzot
2 eggs
1 onion, grated and fried in 2
tablespoons (2½T) chicken fat
salt and pepper
2–3 tablespoons (2½–3¾T) matzo
meal
makes about 24.

Dip the matzot in cold water and squeeze dry. Beat till smooth and add the eggs, onion, seasoning and sufficient matzo meal to bind together. Shape into small balls. Chill if possible.
Cook in boiling, salted water for 15 minutes.

Matzo meal bake

2 eggs
6 tablespoons (7½T) warm water
2 tablespoons (2½T) chicken fat
or margarine
salt and pepper
4 oz. (1 cup) medium
matzo meal

Beat the eggs, adding the water and fat. Add the seasonings and matzo meal. Mix well, adding more water, if necessary, to make a thick batter. Pour into a well greased 1 pint (2½ cup) pie dish. Bake for 45 minutes in the oven at 375°F, Mark 5.
Serve cut in slices with meat, or as a soup accompaniment.

Charoseth

4 tablespoons (5T) chopped nuts
(walnuts, hazelnuts or almonds)
1 small cooking apple, grated
1 teaspoon cinnamon
a little wine

Mix all the ingredients together and bind into a paste with the wine. Form into a flat round shape and serve on the Seder Dish.

Jaffa fluff

1½ oz. (⅜ cup) potato
flour (starch)
½ pint (1¼ cups) water
rind and juice of 1 lemon
rind and juice of 1 orange
2 oz. (¼ cup) sugar
pinch of salt
½ oz. (1T) margarine
2 eggs, separated
nuts to decorate

serves 2–3.

Blend the potato flour (starch) with a little water and juice to make a thin cream. Bring the rest of water, rinds and juices, sugar, salt and margarine to the boil. Pour over the blended potato flour (starch). Return the mixture to the pan and cook for 1 minute. Cool slightly. Add to the beaten egg yolks, and add more sugar or lemon juice if necessary. When cool, fold in the stiffly beaten egg whites. Pour into glass dishes and decorate with nuts.

Plava

3 eggs
4 oz. castor (superfine) sugar
grated rind and juice of ¼ lemon
1 tablespoon (1¼T) water
1 tablespoon (1¼T) oil
2½ oz. fine matzo meal or potato
flour (starch), or a mixture of
both (just over ½ cup)
pinch of salt

Whisk the egg yolks and sugar together until thick. Add the lemon juice and rind, water and oil, and beat well. Fold in the matzo meal and/or potato flour (sifted). Whip the egg whites with the salt until very stiff, and fold into mixture. Pour into 8 in. greased tin lined with greased greaseproof paper at the bottom and sprinkled with ½ teaspoon matzo meal. Bake in the oven at 375°F, Mark 5, for 30 minutes.

Lemon meringue

½ pint (1¼ cups) water
pinch of salt
grated rind of 1 lemon
1 oz. (2T) margarine
1 oz. (⅛ cup) sugar
1½ oz. (⅜ cup) potato
flour (starch)
juice of 2 lemons
3 eggs, separated
Plava baked in 8 in. deep
ovenproof dish
3 oz. (⅜ cup) sugar

Bring the water, salt, lemon rind, margarine and 1 oz. (⅛ cup) sugar to the boil. Blend the potato flour (starch) and lemon juice together. Pour the boiling water mixture over the blended potato flour (starch). Return to the pan, and cook thoroughly. Taste and add more sugar or lemon juice if necessary. Cool a little and add to egg yolks and beat well. Spread over the plava.
Beat egg whites until very stiff, and gradually beat in 3 oz. (⅜ cup) sugar. Pile over the lemon filling, and decorate with almonds if liked. Bake in the oven at 350°F, Mark 4, for 10 minutes until pale brown or in a slower oven at 300°F, Mark 2, for ½ hour.

Orange cake

1 orange
8 oz. (1 cup) sugar
5 eggs
4 oz. (1 cup) fine matzo meal

Wash the orange and cover with water. Bring to the boil, and pour away the water, recovering with fresh water. Bring to the boil and then simmer until tender, about 30 minutes; mash orange (removing pips) or liquidize. Place the sugar in a mixing bowl and warm through in the oven. (Use an ovenproof bowl.) Add the eggs to the sugar and whisk until very thick.
Fold in matzo meal and orange pulp very gently, using a metal spoon. Place in an 8 in. spring form tin, greased and sprinkled with meal. Bake in the oven at 350°F, Mark 4, for 45 minutes.

Carrot pudding

2 oz. (4T) margarine
2 oz. (¼ cup) sugar
2 eggs, separated
2 oz. (scant ½ cup) potato
flour (starch)
1 teaspoon cinnamon
8 oz. (2 cups) carrot, grated
1 tablespoon (1¼T)
walnuts, chopped
4 tablespoons (5T) wine
rind and juice of 1 lemon
1 oz. (⅛ cup) dates, chopped, if
available for Pesach pinch
of salt
serves 4–5.

Cream together the margarine and sugar. Beat in the egg yolks. Fold in the potato flour. Fold in the cinnamon, carrots, walnuts, wine, lemon rind and juice, and dates if available. Whisk the egg whites with salt until very stiff. Fold into the mixture. Bake in a greased oven dish for 45 minutes at 350°F, Mark 4.

Almond pudding

3 eggs
4 oz. (½ cup) castor
(superfine) sugar
3 oz. (¾ cup) ground almonds
serves 4.

Whisk the egg yolks and sugar together until thick and creamy. Fold in the ground almonds. Whisk the egg whites until stiff and fold in gently. Transfer to a greased, 1½ pint (4 cup) pie dish. Bake in the oven at 350°F, Mark 4, for 45 minutes.
Serve immediately after the pudding is removed from the oven.

Apple dessert

4 oz. (1 cup) medium
matzo meal
2 oz. (¼ cup) sugar
½ teaspoon ground cinnamon
2 eggs, beaten
2 oz. (4T) melted butter
or margarine
8 oz. (2 medium sized) cooking
apples, grated
grated rind and juice of ½ lemon
a little water, if necessary
extra sugar
extra butter or margarine

Mix the matzo meal, sugar and cinnamon together. Add the beaten eggs, melted fat, apples and lemon rind and juice. Mix well, adding water, if necessary, to make a soft consistency. Transfer to a greased, 1½ pint (4 cup) pie dish, sprinkle with sugar and dot with butter or margarine. Bake in the oven at 375°F, Mark 5, for 1 hour.

Chocolate refrigerator gâteau

6 oz. (¾ cup) margarine
6 oz. (¾ cup) castor
(superfine) sugar
2 eggs, separated
1 oz. (¼ cup) cocoa
pinch of salt
6 matzot
about ¼ pint (½ cup+2T) of wine
grated chocolate for decoration
blanched almonds
for decoration

Cream together the margarine and sugar until very soft. Beat in the egg yolks and sifted cocoa. Beat the egg whites and salt until very stiff, and fold into mixture. Place 1 matzot on a sheet of foil, moisten well with wine, and spread with the chocolate mixture. Repeat the process until all the matzot are used up ending with a layer of cream; spread the rest of the cream around the sides. Decorate with grated chocolate and blanched almonds.
Chill in the refrigerator, but remove ½ hour before serving.

Cinnamon balls

2 egg whites
4 oz. (½ cup) castor (superfine) sugar
8 oz. (2 cups) ground almonds
1 tablespoon (1¼T) cinnamon
sifted icing (confectioners') sugar

makes about 2 dozen.

Beat the egg whites until very stiff. Beat in 2 oz. (¼ cup) castor (superfine) sugar. Fold in the rest of the sugar, almonds and cinnamon. Roll into small balls. Place on a greased tin and bake in the oven at 400°F, Mark 6, for 10–15 minutes. Roll in icing (confectioner's) sugar while still warm.

Macaroons

1 egg white
4 oz. (1 cup) ground almonds
4 oz. (½ cup) castor (superfine) sugar
1 teaspoon fine matzo meal

makes about 18.

Beat the egg white until fairly stiff. Mix the almonds, sugar and meal together. Add the egg white to form a dough, and form small balls about the size of a walnut. Place on a greased tin a little apart, and flatten. Bake in the oven at 400°F, Mark 6, for 10–15 minutes approximately. If liked, half a blanched almond can be placed on each macaroon before baking. They should be very lightly cooked.

Coconut biscuits

4 oz. (8T) margarine
3 oz. (⅜ cup) sugar
1 egg
3 oz. (¾ cup) matzo meal
6 oz. (2¼ scant cups) desiccated coconut
extra coconut and sugar for coating, equal amounts mixed together

makes about 20 biscuits.

Cream together the margarine and sugar. Add the egg, and beat well. Add the meal and coconut, and mix well. Roll into balls the size of a walnut. Roll each in coconut and sugar, and place on a greased tin and press with a fork. Bake in the oven on greased tin at 350°F, Mark 4, for ½ hour.

Lemon biscuits

4 oz. (8T) margarine
4 oz. (½ cup) castor (superfine) sugar
1 egg
grated rind and juice of ½ lemon
3 oz. (¾ cup) fine matzo meal
2 oz. (½ cup) potato flour (starch)
4 oz. (1 cup) ground almonds

makes about 2 dozen.

Cream together the margarine and sugar. Add the egg, lemon juice and rind. Fold in the meal, potato flour (starch) and almonds. Roll into small balls, and flatten each with a fork. Bake in the oven on a greased tin at 350°F, Mark 4, for ½ hour.
This mixture can be rolled out between two sheets of greaseproof paper and used to make jam tarts or apple pie.

Hazelnut torte

4 eggs
4 oz. (½ cup) castor (superfine) sugar
4 oz. (1 cup) ground hazelnuts or walnuts
1 oz. (¼ cup) medium matzo meal
pinch of salt

Whisk the egg yolks and sugar together until thick and creamy. Fold in the chopped nuts and matzo meal. Whip the egg whites and salt until very stiff and fold in carefully into the yolk mixture. Pour into a 7 in. cake tin, with the base lined with greased greaseproof paper, and sprinkled with 1 teaspoon matzo meal. Bake in the oven at 375°F, Mark 5, for 45 minutes.

Festival of Weeks

In early summer the synagogue is decorated with flowers, foliage and fruits to mark Shavuoth—to commemorate the giving of the Law to Moses on Mount Sinai. Shavuot is also the time of the wheat festival in Israel, hence the flowers and fruit. Milk foods are traditionally served at Shavuoth and cheese blintzes, cheese cakes and tarts abound.

Cheese cake

½ oz. (1T) margarine or butter
5 digestive-type (graham crackers) biscuits
4 oz. (8T) margarine or butter
4 oz. (½ cup) sugar
½ teaspoon vanilla essence
1 teaspoon lemon juice
2 eggs
1 lb. (2⅔ cups) curd cheese
2 level tablespoons (2½T) self raising flour
4 tablespoons (5T) top-of-the-milk [light cream]
½ pint (1¼ cups) sour cream
1 tablespoon (1¼T) sugar, optional

Grease an 8 in. loose bottomed tin very well. Sprinkle with grated biscuits. Cream the fat and sugar together. Beat in the vanilla and lemon juice. Beat in the eggs. Beat in the curd cheese and sifted flour. Beat in the top-of-the-milk (light cream). Place in the prepared tin and bake on the middle shelf of the oven at 350°F, Mark 4, for 1¼–1½ hours until set. Turn off the oven and leave cake to cool. Mix the sour cream and sugar together and spread over the cool cake. Refrigerate until served.

Ripened sheaves of wheat, leaves and flowers (Shavuoth)

Weights and measures
American measures

All recipes in this book are based on Imperial weights and measures, with American equivalents in parentheses.

Measures in weight in the Imperial and American systems are the same.

Measures in volume are different, and the following tables show the equivalents:

spoon measures: Level spoon measurements are used throughout the book.

imperial	american
1 teaspoon (5 ml) (tsp)	$1\frac{1}{4}$ teaspoons
1 tablespoon (20 ml) (tbsp)	$1\frac{1}{4}$ tablespoons (abbrev: T)

liquid measures:

imperial	american	
20 fluid oz.	16 fluid oz.	1 pint
10 fluid oz.	8 fluid oz.	1 cup

metric measures

The following table shows both an exact conversion from Imperial to metric measures and the recommended working equivalent.

weight:

imperial oz.	metric grams	working equivalent grams
1	28.35	25
2	56.7	50
4	113.4	100
8	226.8	200
12	340.2	300
1.0 lb	453	400
1.1 lb	$\frac{1}{2}$ kilo	
2.2 lb	1 kilo	

liquid measures:

imperial	exact conversion	working equivalent
$\frac{1}{4}$ pint (1 gill)	142 millilitres	150 ml
$\frac{1}{2}$ pint	284 ml	300 ml
1 pint	568 ml	600 ml
$1\frac{3}{4}$ pints	994 ml	1 litre

linear measures:

1 inch	$2\frac{1}{2}$ cm
2 inch	5 cm
3 inch	$7\frac{1}{2}$ cm
6 inch	15 cm

It is useful to note for easy reference that:
1 kilogramme (1000 grammes) = 2.2 lb therefore
$\frac{1}{2}$ kilo (500 grammes) roughly = 1 lb
1 litre roughly = $1\frac{3}{4}$ Imperial pints therefore
$\frac{1}{2}$ litre roughly = 1 Imperial pint

Oven temperatures

In this book oven temperatures are given in degrees Fahrenheit with the equivalent Gas mark number. The following chart gives the conversions from degrees Fahrenheit to degrees Centigrade:

°F	°C	
225	110	very cool or very slow
250	130	
275	140	cool or slow
300	150	
325	170	very moderate
350	180	moderate
375	190	moderately hot
400	200	
425	220	hot
450	230	very hot
475	240	

Glossary of Jewish cooking terms

bagel	Traditional yeast roll with a hole in the centre, first boiled and then baked.
blintzes	Thin pancakes filled and folded parcel-like.
bola	A cut of Kosher forequarter meat.
challah	Plaited Sabbath Loaf.
einbren	A brown roux made by cooking flour with fat until a light-brown.
essigfleisch	Sweet and sour meat.
farfel	Noodle dough which is coarsely grated and used as soup garnish.
gedempte fleisch	Stewed meat.
grieven	Cracklings from rendered chicken fat.
kasha	Buckwheat.
kneidlach	Dumplings, often made with matzo meal.
knishes	Baked stuffed patties.
kreplach	Kosher 'Ravioli'. A type of dough, boiled, fried with a tasty filling, usually savoury.
kugel	Any baked pudding.
latkes	A kind of pancake-cum-fritter made with grated raw potato or sometimes matzo meal and egg.
lekach	Honey cake.
lochshen	Noodles.
matzo	Unleavened bread, bought from delicatessens and Jewish grocers.
matzo meal	Finely ground unleavened bread.
parve cream	A non-dairy cream substitute commonly available in Jewish delicatessens.
pirogen or piroshki	See Kreplach.
smetana	Soured milk, specially cultured, often with added cream, available at most good delicatessens and health food shops.
strudel	A very thin pastry dough, filled and tightly rolled up—either sweet or savoury.
tayglach	Snippets of pastry cooked in honey.
tschav	Sorrel soup
tzimmes	Meat and carrots cooked in honey.
varenikes	See Kreplach.
worsht	A smoked Continental sausage, served in slices and often uncooked. Available from Kosher butchers and delicatessens.

Sources of information

Union of Orthodox Jewish Congregations of America, Kashrus Division, 84, Fifth Avenue, New York, NY 1001, USA.

O.K. Laboratories, 105, Hudson Street, New York, NY 10013, USA.

Melbourne Beth Din, Kashrus Department, Synagogue Chambers, Toorak Road, South Yarra, 3141 Melbourne, Victoria, Australia.

Sydney Beth Din and New South Wales, Kashrus Commission, 140 Darlinghurst Road, Darlinghurst NW11 2010, New South Wales, Australia.

Beth Din, 5491 Victoria Avenue 26, Montreal, Quebec, Canada.

Beth Din Johannesburg, 24 Raleigh Street, Yeoville, Johannesburg, South Africa.

Beth Din Cape Town, P.O. Box 543, Cape Town, South Africa.

Beth Din London, (Court of the Chief Rabbi), Adler House, Tavistock Square, London, WC1H 9HP.

London Board for Shechita, Oceanair House, 133–137 Whitechapel High Street, London, E1 7QG.

Kashrus Commission, Woburn House, Upper Woburn Place, London, WC1.

Manchester Beth Din and Shechita Board, 435 Cheetham Hill Road, Manchester 8.

Leeds Beth Din and Shechita Board, 98 Chapeltown Road, Leeds 7.

Belfast Shechita Board, Synagogue Somerton Road, Belfast, Northern Ireland.

General Board of Shechita of Eire, Zion Schools, Bloomfield Road, Dublin 8, Eire.

Joint Kashrus Commission, Union of Orthodox Hebrew Congregation, Queen Elizabeth Walk, London, N16.

Southend and Westcliff Shechita Board, Synagogue Finchley Road, Westcliff.

Edinburgh Shechita Board, Synagogue 4, Salisbury Road, Edinburgh Scotland.

Gateshead-on-Tyne Shechita Board, 180 Berwick Road, Gateshead 8.

Glasgow Beth Din, Falloch Road, Glasgow S.2, Scotland.

Liverpool Board of Shechita, 262 Parliament Street, Liverpool 8.

Cardiff Board of Shechita, The Synagogue, Cathedral Road, Cardiff.

Birmingham Shechita Board, Singers Hill, Birmingham.

Jewish Marriage Education Council, Cookery and Home Management Department, 529b, Finchley Road, London, NW3.

Acknowledgements

The following colour photographs are by courtesy of:

John Searle Austin: Halibut with Egg and Lemon Sauce (p. 34); Savoury Vegetable Strudel (p. 65); Pesach Puffs (p. 127); Plava (p. 127); Macaroons (p. 7); Cinnamon Balls (p. 7); Coconut Biscuits (p. 7); Cholent (p. 7); Gefillte Fish (p. 35); Apple Strudel (p. 90).

Australian Recipe Service: Continental Fruit Cake (p. 82); Kiddush Sultana Cake (p. 94–5); Yeasty Fruit Cake (p. 83); Strudel for Succoth (p. 127); Schnecken (p. 90); Iced Almond Ring (p. 82).

Barretware Kichlen (p. 86); Mandelbrot (p. 86); Cinnamon Biscuits (p. 86); Wine Biscuits (p. 86); Nuss Kichlen (p. 86); Eier Kichlen (p. 86).

Cadbury-Schweppes (Hartleys) Kissel (p. 76–7).

Canned & Packaged Foods Bureau Spiced Fish (p. 35); Goulash (p. 42–3); Fruit Salad (p. 127).

Fruit Producers Council Apple Shalet (p. 68); Apple Cake (p. 69); Apple Pie (p. 72).

Jewish Marriage Education Council Eve of Sabbath Table Setting (p. 119); Sabbath Meal (p. 122–3).

Jobling Housecraft Service Avocado Dip (p. 115); Houmous (p. 115); Pickled Cucumbers (p. 114); Red Cabbage (p. 114).

Lawry's Foods International Veal Casserole with Dumplings (p. 38–9).

Pentangle Photography Cheesecake (p. 7); Avocado Soup (p. 15); Cheese Chocolate Triangle (p. 83); Schwarzwalde (p. 87); Purim Kalisch (p. 94); Boobelach (p. 115).

Potato Marketing Board Rossel Fleisch and Potato Latkes (p. 43); Baked Worsht Potatoes (p. 46).

Pasta Foods Ltd (Avery's) Lochshen Pudding (p. 73).

Rice Council Roast Duck (p. 46); Braised Liver, Mushrooms and Rice (p. 46).

The Tupperware Co Pflummencompote, Parve Fruit Fools (p. 80).

Paf International (Christian Délu) Moussaka (p. 47); Kol Bo Salad with Sour Cream (p. 65).

Tupperware Kneidlach (p. 15); Kasha (p. 15); Mandlen (p. 15); Orange and Chicory Salad (p. 65); Celery, Apple and Walnut Salad (p. 65); Marble Angel Cake (p. 94); Fruit Balls (p. 114); Pomerantzen (p. 114); Stuffed Dates and Prunes (p. 114); Aubergine (Eggplant), Eggs and Onions (p. 11); Chopped Herring (p. 11); Mushrooms in Smetana (p. 11); Aubergine Pâté (p. 11); Herring Salad (p. 11); Eggs and Onion (p. 11); Avocado Surprise with Tuna Fish and Cream Cheese (p. 14).

John West Pineapple Cheesecake (p. 91).

Black and white photographs by courtesy of:

John Searle Austin Buckling (p. 20); Schwartz Retaych (p. 19); Petcha (p. 18); Smetana Soup (p. 25); Salmon Patties (p. 36); Boiled Ox Tongue (p. 53); Stuffed Chicken Neck (Helzel) (p. 52); Stuffed Aubergine (p. 57); Cherry Slices (p. 74); Cous Cous (p. 79); Baklava (p.81); Kuchen (p. 101); Cheese Buns (p. 93); Kiddush Chocolate Cake (p. 97); Honey Cake Lekach (p. 124); Holishkes (p. 129).

Australian Recipe Service Stuffed Monkey (p. 93).

Canned & Packaged Foods Bureau Sweet and Sour Mackerel (p. 33); Lentil Soup (p. 23); Sweet and Sour Cabbage Borsht with Raisins (p. 23); Einbren of Peas and Carrots (p. 62); Pineapple, Celery and Walnut Salad (p. 63); Asparagus Soup (p. 24); Split Pea and Worsht Soup (p. 24).

Flour Advisory Bureau Bread Kneidlach (p. 28); Stuffed Breast of Lamb (p. 50); Date and Honey Pudding (p. 75); Bread Pudding (p. 71); Kugelhof (p. 99); Kipfel (p. 88).

Herring Industry Board Soused Herring (p. 37).

Jobling Housecraft Service Schwemelach and Barley Soup (p. 26); Salmon Rolls (p. 113); Curd Cheese Biscuits (p. 113); Onion Biscuits (p. 113).

John West Tuna Fish Cocktail (p. 17); Tuna and Egg Roll (p. 56).

Lawry's Foods International Braised Bola (p. 41).

Pasta Foods Ltd (Avery's) Lochshen Kaese and Puter (p. 55); Lochshen Kaese Kugel (p. 55).

Potato Marketing Board Grated Potato Kugel (p. 60); Potato Pudding (Kugel) (p. 56); Kol Bo Salad (p. 60).

RHM Foods Ltd Bridge Rolls (p. 116).

The Gas Council Mustard Casserole (p. 40); Pepper Holishkes (p. 49); Challah (p. 120).

Van Den Bergh's Tomor Gedempte Fleisch (p. 41); Rouladen (p. 44); Almond Biscuits (p. 89); Almond Cake (p. 102); Linzer Torte (p. 105).

Vic Kettle Studios Hamantaschen (p. 133).

White Fish Authority Baked Stuffed Fish (p. 32).

Index